For
Audrie Gardner
at Steinbeck Festival X
Bruce Ariss
8/L/89

Inside Cannery Row

Sketches from the Steinbeck Era
in words and pictures

First edition
Copyright © 1988 Bruce Ariss

All rights reserved. No part of this book may be produced in any form by any electronic or mechanical means, including information storage and retrieval systems, without permission in writing from the publisher.

Published by Lexikos

Edited by Laurie Cohn and Mike Witter

Design and Production by Mark Adamsbaum

Front mural by Bruce Ariss, © 1984 Monterey Bay Aquarium.

Mural photo by Geoffrey Johnson.

Photo of end papers by Beauford Fisher.

Author photo by Claus-Michael Naske.

Set in 10 point Bookman. Reproduced from pages generated on the Macintosh II computer and printed on the Apple LaserWriter printer.

ISBN 0-938530-45-3

Printed in the United States of America

DEDICATION

TO JEAN FITCH ARISS

Talented golden girl of the 30s, who remembers these hectic and pleasant adventures as well as I do, but who, if she'd wished, could have written them (from her quite different point of view) with much more expertise than I.

ACKNOWLEDGEMENTS

To Bill Brandon, Bob Herhold, Barney Inada, and Evvy Londahl Larson, good friends, who needled me to get started on this project.

To Doc Etienne, who insisted that I finish it, and who supplied his gracious secretary, Nancy Nawrocki Gams, to put all these hen-scratched ramblings down neatly on a marvelous machine called a word processor.

To Geoffrey Johnson of Oakland, who took the fine color photo of my mural on the cover, reproduced here through the courtesy of the Monterey Bay Aquarium. To Sybil Anakiev of Carmel, who took the photo of the Cannery murals on the back cover. To Beauford Fisher of Pacific Grove, who took the photo of the WPA mural on the end papers, and to Russ Cummings, best of friends and incomparable photographer who took the photo of my Monterey Mural, as well as the great color photo of Ellwood Graham's Steinbeck portrait on the back cover. To my son-in-law Claus-Michael Naske for his constant encouragement, and who took time off from his own busy writing career to locate a publisher for this volume and who took the picture of me on the back cover; to my lovely daughter, Holly, who typed many of the final corrections.

To Jean Ariss, who's put up with me for more than fifty years—and in particular, while I was preoccupied with this project—but without whom this book wouldn't have been written. Jean has sworn she'll never read it and so far hasn't. She feels too much has been written about John already. Besides, Jean has always recalled things differently than I have, is a far better writer than I, and, like John, has always been outspoken against authorial collaboration. She feared that, in our case, even a fine fifty year marriage might not survive one.

"*Cannery Row's Working Girls*"   Monterey, 1936

CONTENTS

I   The Riches of the Depression   page 2

II   Travels With Steinbeck   page 31

III   Cannery Row Revisited   page 71

FOREWORD

IN THE 1930s John Steinbeck, a relatively hungry young California writer, was developing into the foremost author of the American Depression. He had grown up in the central part of the State, in Monterey County, and by the end of that decade the four or five provocative novels he had written in and about this area had precipitated him into worldwide recognition.

John Steinbeck, like most important writers, was a spokesman for his time. His early works were largely inspired by an angry compassion for the "Little People" of this world who'd been the victims of an enormous economic disaster. This book will have as much to say about the Depression that formed him (and his generation) as it will about Steinbeck himself.

In this book I propose to go back to examine the earlier, vital, and colorful days in Monterey, and show how Steinbeck's local surroundings, combined with the hard times and all his day-to-day personal problems, helped him produce his finest literary work.

In particular, I'd like to describe a 1936 trip we took to Baja, that long desolate peninsula that lies west of the Mexican mainland. This journey was made by motorcar, some four years before the 1940 expedition by boat that Steinbeck was to document in the *Sea of Cortez*.

This land trip was undertaken for the same reason as the later sea voyage. We were collecting marine specimens for Steinbeck's best friend, Ed Ricketts, who was referred to as "Doc," and for the little Pacific Biological Lab he operated on the Cannery Row waterfront.

It was to be a pleasant trip, full of sunshine and good conversation, just as the ordinary day for our little group on the Row seemed to be. This trip was to provide me the opportunity to isolate Steinbeck from the distractions of his overzealous fans so that I could talk to him on an uninterrupted one-to-one basis. If possible, with these rambling recollections, I'd like to take everyone along with me on that trip, back into that Depression time, back into that lost microcosm of a special Monterey era. It was a time that today, more than fifty years later, survives mostly in the memories of the few old-timers like myself who are left in this area.

The real Cannery Row of the sardine canning days has disappeared, of course, along with the sardines themselves. Only a facsimile of false fronts remains of the canneries, preserved or refabricated for the benefit of the ever-present tourists and Steinbeck devotees. And the fictional Row, as portrayed in the author's two short novels, is a figment, a myth, an illusion, a distorted funhouse mirror version of the original reality of a street that might best be described as an industrial slumway. *Cannery Row* and *Sweet Thursday* were written by Steinbeck more or less as divertissements between his other more serious and substantial novels.

In this Foreword I first better introduce the small cast of characters, the four of us, who made that 1936 Baja trip:

Ed, John, my young wife, Jean, and myself. Ed's little laboratory on Cannery Row, at that time, provided samples of flora and fauna from the Pacific Coast's tidepools mainly to college classrooms around the world.

Over the years literary history buffs have plagued me to let them tape my recollections of this trip, and of the good old Steinbeck-Ricketts days of Cannery Row. I've consistently refused. If I hadn't, this first-hand account already would be second-hand. However, I like the concept of someone taping his youthful memories, in free association, and have used such a format.

Primarily, I'm trying to recapture a world that no longer exists. It's a place I see in my mind's eye as clearly now as I first saw it more than fifty years ago. To help me, I have only a sometimes disconcertingly detailed memory, reinforced by the recollections of old friends, and the help of five or six battered spiral-bound sketch books. These are filled with my hastily annotated pencil drawings, dashed off at the time, as I explored amongst the fishing boats and cannery scenes, trying to capture that special quality of the characters who inhabited that now celebrated era.

The interest and curiosity about John's Cannery Row still continues to grow. Ed Ricketts' sister, Frances Strong, told me that in the last few years there were more than ninety masters' and doctoral theses being written about Ed and John and the symbiotic relationship that had helped produce John's literary success. She said most of these researchers asked to tape her recollections. In the last few years of her life, though she was in delicate health, she did her best to oblige them.

Many of them called Jean and me too, but we formulated a ready answer. "We're very sorry, but we're writers, too. If we allow you to tape our first-hand reminiscences, they'll instantly become second-hand, won't they? And any books we might hope to do on the subject would become instantly superfluous."

I must say our device worked. With a few belligerent exceptions, most of these writers understood our position and backed off at once. Those who heard of my sketch books were anxious to see them published. They said they could find few pictures of John and Ed in the Cannery Row days. I explained that it was very likely because in the Depression there were almost no shutterbugs running around, as there are today. People didn't have the money for such an expensive hobby.

Not all the conversations I've recalled are to be considered as word for word, of course. I think I have what the old actor Jimmy Cagney called an "Irish Memory." I can close my eyes and see every detail of some scene, just as it was, fifty or sixty years ago. Jean feels that remembering trivia and describing it in a book, the way Proust did, can become pretty boring. She didn't think that Steinbeck's step-by-step description of Tom Joad's repair job on an old Dodge was particularly interesting. I did. I found it fascinating. It's one of the scenes I remember most vividly in *The Grapes of Wrath*. I believe Steinbeck had an Irish Memory, too.

Personally, I'm no Johnny Bear—the human sound-recording bar-fly in John's fine short story of that name. I never made any tapes. In those days we would have used those thin silvery wires to record conversations. They were difficult to rewind and usually ended up jumping the reels and looping around everything in the room. If I had made recordings, I probably would have lost them by now, anyway. Without them, I can still "re-hear" the sound of Ed's and John's voices. John's was low, husky, gravelly, with lots of chuckling, while Ed's tone was more serious and lighter-timbered, quiet, kindly, and slightly pedantic.

I've taken the liberty of describing most of our conversations in quotes. It was the only way I felt I could recapture, in a natural fashion, the sound and content of those times. Obviously, after fifty years, they can't be word for word, or even in the exact sequence of their happening. Some of the things that were said before or after the trip, for example, may have crept into the Baja discussions, but the words are strictly in character and as close to the originals as I can recall.

In a few instances, I have changed slightly the names

of the people involved in some of the more outlandish episodes on the Row. I felt they, or their surviving relatives, might prefer some small screen of anonymity. In addition, I want to make some excuses for the hasty quality of my Baja sketches. They were mostly done in a great rush, just as notes really, from which I hoped to do more complete works later. (Such as the mural on the jacket of this book, or the end papers of the Monterey coastline WPA mural.)

A good friend of mine, writer Bill Brandon, convinced me that the very casual quality of the Mexican trip sketches was what was important. Bill said they caught the immediacy of a scene, like a snapshot, and were more real because of their half-finished quality.

"Print 'em just like they are," he insisted. He may have a point, and since that's the line of least resistance, I'm taking his advice. I'll make no further apologies for my sketches being sketchy.

SECTION I

THE RICHES OF THE DEPRESSION

FROM ITS ORIGIN in the October '29 collapse on Wall Street, the Depression had smashed its way around the world like an overpowering shock wave. A tsunami-like wall of economic misery had engulfed almost everyone, from captains of industry to their lowliest workers, from bankers to field hands and, of course, to all of their dependents.

Monterey, fortunately, was only tangentially effected by all this. Not that things weren't tough here too, but it wasn't as rugged as it was in the larger, more industrialized cities of the world. We watched those dreary newsreel pictures with queues of wretched people standing half-covered with snow, in the New York or Chicago soup lines. And, of course, there were always those gruesome and seemingly inevitable shots of the corpses of East Indians and Africans, dead of starvation, lying like piles of straw in their streets.

For one thing, the climate of Monterey was relatively mild. The Chamber of Commerce assured us we had the "smallest mean temperature change," from summer to winter, of any place on earth. Since this was a summer resort area, housing was plentiful, particularly in the winter, and quite inexpensive. Ten or fifteen bucks a month would do it. Scrap vegetables could be gleaned from the large truck gardens that surrounded us. Monterey's bay was full of sardines, mackerel, cod, and miscellaneous sea foods of all kinds. And there were some seasonable cannery jobs on the Row for the able-bodied who weren't afraid of hard work.

No doubt the Depression was more of a hardship on older people, who saw their livelihoods and their life savings disappearing, and of course, on invalids, infants, small children, and other economically helpless human beings. However, to my very young wife, to me, and to all our healthy young artist and writer friends on the Monterey Peninsula, the Depression was a challenge that could be met rather successfully on a day to day basis, with optimism, and even with some excitement. As a generation we may have suffered from lack of opportunity in our lives, as sociologists claimed, but we weren't particularly aware of it at the time.

I thought it a strange irony that Steinbeck, through the very act of writing about the Great Depression, was able to extricate himself from its grasp. Three of his outstanding novels of the Depression, *In Dubious Battle*, *Of Mice and Men*, and *The Grapes of Wrath*, were deluging him with so much money that he was losing touch with the dispossessed people of the day, those very same ones who'd been the source of his inspiration and success.

The early 1930s was a time in Steinbeck's life when I knew him best. He was almost at the peak of his powers as a writer, and was still progressing. It was just before he was to move east and lose his generic link to the good black earth of Monterey County; just before he was to divorce his thorny first wife, Carol, and lose the editorial discipline she provided him; and somewhat before the death, in an untimely train accident, of his best friend, Ed Ricketts, who had supplied him with so much of the spiritual and philosophical inspiration which he'd absorbed into his writings.

Although I was then only in my early twenties, I was as intrigued by the excitement, the noise, and the raw vitality of the Row as was my friend, John Steinbeck. He was some ten years my senior. He had been absorbing the feel of the same area to use in his stories for quite a few years before I arrived on the Peninsula.

John was born and raised in Salinas, the County seat, some twenty miles inland. His folks had their summer home near the seacoast, on Eleventh Street, in Pacific Grove, not far from Cannery Row. As a boy, during vacations, Steinbeck clambered over the rocks and tidepools and watched the sardine fishermen and canners at their work.

I came to Pacific Grove in 1934, a literature and art school graduate, with Jean, a talented young poet, writer, and my teen aged bride. We were on our honeymoon and were so delighted with the Peninsula that we've never really left it. I made sketches as background notes for a 150-foot long WPA mural I was preparing to paint on the walls of the Pacific Grove High School library. By a happy insight, I decided that painting another standard mural of early Spanish settlers dancing the fandango would be less important than depicting the vigorous, and probably transitory, life on Cannery Row.

No doubt with a similar insight, a decade later, Steinbeck was to write his famous novel, *Cannery Row*. It is filled with his sprightly fiction about the "bums and saints" who, because of the power of his prose, have since become more real than the actual inhabitants of that Depression day street were themselves. Even as John was writing his book, the sardines were in the process of being fished out of existence. Today the cannery buildings' shells, with their restored facades, are all that remain.

The street is now populated by armies of tourists searching for Steinbeck's fantasy, and by all the restaurateurs and shopkeepers necessary to operate the booming service industry that has developed to exploit them.

Long before his death, Steinbeck realized the irony of this scene. Tongue in cheek, he suggested that the application of synthetic fish odors and plastic blowflies would make the now touristy Row more authentic, and more true to the really revolting atmosphere of those earlier days.

When my wife Jean and I first met him in Ed Ricketts' little waterfront laboratory, Steinbeck was just another struggling, discouraged, but no longer quite so young writer.

He had ambled into Ed's place, out of the fog of Cannery Row, or Ocean View Avenue, as it was called then. He was a hulking figure in his loose-fitting brown corduroy trousers, heavy boots, and enormous, sheepskin-lined canvas coat. The shaggy collar was turned up around his large, cold reddened ears. He was bareheaded. Drops of moisture glistened in his hair, which was short, dark, and rather thin, but wiry and curly. He had a receding hairline, a beefy complexion, rather corpulent features, pale blue eyes, and a crooked apologetic grin. He had two or three days' growth of dark whiskers on his heavy jowls, but his thin mustache was carefully trimmed. Somehow, because of that mustache, I assumed he was not just another unemployed working stiff who had wandered in off the street to get warm.

Ed introduced us informally and served us some hot tea, lightly spiked with rum. He noted that the three of us should have plenty to talk about, since we were all interested in writing. Then he excused himself, and retreated to his basement laboratory, where he was in the process of embalming some cats for an order.

That day we first met, in November or December 1934, was a time when John was not very well known. At least we had never heard of him before, so he rather diffidently began to tell us about himself. After ten years of scribbling, he had only a few short stories published in small magazines. Nothing much, really, but he had been lucky enough to have two of his novels published. We were immediately impressed, but he was self-deprecatory about that, too.

"Unfortunately," he chuckled in his heavy, apologetic, and lugubrious fashion, "They were actually terrible duds."

The novels were such failures, he told us, that both of their separate publishers instantly had gone bankrupt. John considered himself a bad-luck writer, a literary Jonah, an auctorial albatross ready to be hung around the neck of the next unwary publisher to come his way.

He may have meant this as a warning, since I had just told him that I was working as an underpaid editor on a

Doc's Lab

miserable little magazine called the *Monterey Beacon*. If so, his warning was unnecessary, I told him, since the *Beacon* was moribund anyway. I'd taken it over from an eccentric publisher who became bored with it and had gone into boarding horses. I cherished some rather juvenile hopes from my college magazine days that I could infuse it with literary vitality and perhaps make it pay us back something for all the work we'd put into it.

According to John's biography, he had three books published by this time: *Cup of Gold*, 1929; *Pastures of Heaven*, 1932; and *To a God Unknown*, 1933, but for some reason, he told us he had only two published. Why, I don't know. False modesty, perhaps? That seems unlikely. Although John often put on an abashed schoolboy type of diffidence to hide his obvious egotism, he was usually quite proud of his achievements. They were already notable in those difficult days of the Depression writing game. Perhaps he only mentioned the two because it made a better story to say all of his publishers had failed because of his books, instead of two out of three.

In any case, John's beginning success at writing, for that time, was exceptional. All across the country there were thousands of unemployed men and women plugging away at their typewriters, dreaming of sudden fame and riches from the publication of short stories or novels. Like the lotteries, the dreams gave a bit of hope to many of the hopeless.

One of the biggest problems for writers was scraping up enough postage to send manuscripts to and from the publishers. Hard earned nickels and dimes from jobs washing dishes or from the WPA went to the mailman, who only seemed to bring back standard and impersonal rejection slips:

> The editors regret that your manuscript does not suit the requirements of publication at this time, etc., etc.

Occasionally one of my wife's short stories would earn a personal comment from a reader or editor, which at least was encouraging. One reader had pencilled "Possible" on her story but a higher up had added "Impossible." At the time, we felt quite set up because we realized that at least two living people had read it. Disgruntled writers told us stories about agents or publishers who put manuscripts in a dry washing machine and agitated them so it would appear they had been read.

Many fledgling writers papered the walls above their typewriters with their rejection slips. John told us he had done that in his early days, but they became too depressing, and one day in a fit of anger, he tore them all down and threw them in the wastebasket.

I remember seeing a photo in *Harper's* magazine, in the 1930s, of the huge stack of manuscripts submitted for their Novel of the Year award. It was a pile about the size of a small automobile. Difficult to imagine all the sweat and hopes in those massed bundles of pages!

Jean had worked beside me on the little *Beacon* magazine, albeit reluctantly. She was much more realistic about it than I. She thought we were wasting valuable time on the *Beacon*, time we could have better spent hiking through the hills and along the seashore. Or we could have been working on our own short stories, or I could have been stretching canvases and painting oils or watercolors.

Jean and I primed the little *Beacon* with all our own rejection slipped short stories, mostly under pseudonyms. It made it appear we had a large stable of contributors. I illustrated the magazine generously with linoleum block engravings.

I subtitled the *Beacon* "The Literary Magazine of the West." To our surprise, it began to receive favorable notices from national writers' magazines, who described it as a "Prestigious Showcase for New Writers." Mainly through these notices we attracted some of the better younger writers of the county, namely Bill Hogan, Paul Nathan, Vardis Fisher, and a few others who donated some of their rejected stories to us. Remo, a Carmel sculptor friend, said Bill Saroyan was a good friend of his and would send some of his rejects. In those days, just seeing his work in print was often a young writer's only reward. "Showcasing in the Beacon," we implied editorially, "would inevitably lead to a lucrative discovery by big national magazines."

As far as I know, the only one of our writers this ever happened to was John Steinbeck. He'd given us one of his "unsalable" short stories entitled, *A Snake of One's Own*. He was paid for it with a beat up old Western saddle and all the free riding time he wanted from the boarding stables run in conjunction with the printing press. The snake story was reprinted in *Esquire* some three years later, in 1938, under its shortened title, *The Snake*. It also appeared later that same year in John's collection of short

Ed in Lab basement 1935

stories, *The Long Valley*.

Since Jean and I had a low budget, Ed sent us down to Hovden Cannery to see a friend of his in the labeling department. The one pound cans, being oval shaped, were difficult to wrap with their long, garish paper strip labels. The machine was rather thumb handed, too. It frequently .oused up, tortured the cans, and flung them all over the place in fits of mechanical frenzy and frustration. When this happened, the operator stopped the machine as quickly as he could and picked up the bent and mangled cans. If they weren't punctured by the steel fingers he put them into cardboard boxes of twenty-four each, under the table, and sold them for 50¢ a box on the black market. A little over two cents a can! That was well within our bite sized budget. Old Henry David Thoreau would have been ecstatic over such a bargain.

Monterey canned sardines were large, six inches long without their heads and tails, coarse textured, and rather rank smelling. They were rich in vitamins and very filling, but they became cloying after a steady diet of them. Most were packed in a gummy tomato sauce that was almost as odorous as the fish. Some were packed in a more tasty mustard sauce, or in linseed oil, and we were always delighted when we opened up one of the unlabeled damaged cans and found it to be one of these more palatable variations.

Jean eventually refused to eat any more sardines because, she said, she'd become allergic to the smell of them. If she took three deep breaths in the morning while opening a tin, she didn't feel like eating anything for the rest of the day.

Once she put an opened can I couldn't finish outside on the ground for the neighbor's cat. He ran up to it, inhaled, and backed off stiff legged. Then he turned around and scratched dirt through his hind legs over it. Our local newspaper editor, a well to do society man, suggested in an editorial that Monterey's poor people could aid the general economy, and their own, by eating more of this inexpensive local product. He received a batch of Letters to the Editor daring him to try a steady diet of the medicine he prescribed for others.

Before we started our big family we often visited Ed Ricketts in the bay side yard of his laboratory, where he distilled shark liver oil, boiling it down to a syrup that was dark brown and nasty smelling. He sold it for a pet foot additive, but drank it religiously himself. He tried to get Jean and me to do the same. He said we'd never catch colds if we each took a tablespoonful a day. We tried, but it tasted so god-awful we told him we'd prefer to have the colds.

Once we went on a shark hunt with Ed on Monterey Bay, or rather, we stayed on shore to help the sharkhunters in their small motorboat. They harpooned two massive basking sharks, each twenty feet long. A half dozen of us on the beach hauled in the sharks. They were black and fierce looking, but Ed said they were harmless, not predatory, and besides, they were dead from the harpoons by the time they were pulled into the surf.

We helped roll them up on the beach and watched Ed cut out the huge livers. After the livers were removed, the motorboat towed the sharks out to sea again and cut them adrift. I presume they washed up on some other distant beach, later on. Their skins were covered with millions of little needles and we were surprised to see the palms of our hands were criss crossed with myriads of tiny black scratches from tugging on their bristly hides.

People eat shark meat, nowadays, and find it almost as delicious as halibut, but for some reason, it didn't occur to us we were watching several tons of good, edible meat drift out to sea.

Soon after we met John, due to the publication of his novel *Tortilla Flat*, his fortunes changed dramatically for the better. Prior to that, he and his leggy, red headed, and hot tempered wife Carol, had been "eeking"—just barely getting by—the way we all did. With the almost immediate popular acclaim of his new novel about the *paisanos* of Monterey, his future seemed assured.

One of the people we knew who claimed credit for Steinbeck's sudden phenomenal success was Fred Bechdolt, the venerable Carmel novelist. Fred had been put in charge of the local chapter of FDR's new Federal Writers Project which, along with a number of other WPA art projects, had been established to keep American artists and writers from starving to death or committing suicide during the black days of the Depression.

John was qualified to go on WPA at the time, but his *Tortilla Flat* was only half finished and he felt that if he could only complete it, it would sell and make Carol and him some money. On the other hand, if he went on the Project, he'd have to shelve the book and then he would probably never get back to it.

John asked Fred Bechdolt if he would put Carol on the Writers Project instead, as she'd be far better than he at the sort of local historical research writing the Project was doing. She typed and edited most of his literary efforts and was damn good at it. More to the point, the salary Carol would bring home could then finance his finishing *Tortilla Flat*, and if it hit the jackpot, they'd be off the government dole forever.

Bechdolt scratched his jaw dubiously. He explained to John that Project rules plainly stated "the male head of the household" was the one required to be employed. He said he had read some of John's published short stories, so he was aware of the young writer's talent.

Fred was no rule book bureaucrat. After some hesitation he decided to hell with it—he'd ignore the stupid requirements. Carol went to work on the Writers Project and John stayed home and continued working on *Tortilla Flat* until it was finished. Fred Bechdolt felt if he had refused John's request that day, it could have put an end to the author's fabulous career before it started.

Hovden's Sardine Can Labeling Machine.

There was a story going around Ed's Lab that Carol wasn't too keen on working at her new job, and that she demanded that John keep writing. John was too gregarious, she said, and loved to "sit around and bullshit." If she was going to work, by God, so was he. No loafing around down at the Lab for him!

John agreed, and we saw very little of him there for a few months. Another part of the story was that in the mornings when she went to work, Carol would lock him into his little chickenshed sized studio in the garden. In the evenings, when she came home, she would let him out again.

The writing shed was only about four feet square, with just enough head room to stand up in. John had put in a large makeshift desk, and hinged a door on the south side. He left it open to the sun on warm days. As far as I recall there never was a lock on the door, so that story about Carol was apocryphal. The same story has been told about other writers, namely Joseph Conrad, whose wife supposedly locked him in his room to write, ignored his hammering and pleading to get out, and even shoved his food in through a trap in the door when he was hungry.

Stories about John being a boozer, a drunk, irresponsible, and a barfly are also untrue. He was serious about his writing and worked hard at it for long hours at a time. When he was tired, naturally he liked to relax and shoot the breeze with his friends. He liked red wine, which was cheap and plentiful in those days. If you brought your own gallon jug to Leidig's down by the S.P. Station, near the City Wharf, they would fill it up from big barrels of Burgundy for 29¢, and give you a free cork to cap it with. After a glass or two, John became convivial, animated, expansive, and told great stories, but I never remember seeing him drunk.

Tortilla Flat was published in May 1935, but its success was not as quick and simple as is now told. Several publishers rejected it, and Covici-Friede, by whom it was eventually accepted, did so with misgivings. Critics panned it, but the public loved it. The sales were phenomenal. It was on the best seller list for months. Money started rolling in, but John and Carol refused to believe their good fortune. They said they fully expected to wake up in the morning and discover it was all a crazy dream, and that they would soon be back "eeking" with the rest of us. In the meantime, they planned to squirrel away all the money they could for the time when their lucky bubble would burst.

A best seller! John had always said the worst thing he could imagine happening to a writer would be to have a best seller. He may have said this partly in jest, or partly in fear of losing his own soul, in case it should happen to him. He was certainly being prophetic, we thought later.

With the overwhelming success of *Tortilla Flat*, Steinbeck found he had become a public property, an American celebrity; a person who was expected to sign autographs and nothing else. Strangers stopped him on the street to shake his hand. They told him they bought his book, a transaction they assumed included an automatic introduction to its author.

Mostly, people pestered him to tell them the whereabouts of the real *Tortilla Flat*. At first he patiently explained that it didn't exist, or, if it did, it was a combination of many places. His public refused to believe it. The magical little paisano world he had created was so real it must exist! Perhaps John Steinbeck was trying to protect the area from sightseers?

Eventually John discovered a very simple answer. He would grin and tap his forehead with his forefinger, meaning it's in my head!

From many sessions sitting around talking with John at the Lab, we pieced together a half dozen or more locations on the Monterey Peninsula that had contributed to John's little world of *Tortilla Flat*. In the first place, he seemed to have picked up some of the stories about the paisanos from an old friend, Sue Gregory, who taught journalism at Monterey High School. Across the quarry gulch from the school, along Johnson Street, there was a row of little paisano shacks (they're all gone now) that we all considered to be the ones that had inspired the first stories about Danny's two inherited houses.

Some of John's detractors, envious of his sudden success, claimed he had taken Sue's stories without her consent. John didn't deign to answer such charges. He dedicated the book to Susan Gregory of Monterey. A friend to both of them, editor Evelyn Londahl Larson, said that Sue had given John the stories freely because she was in ill health and felt he could write the story of the Monterey Paisano, whereas she might never get around to it. Other old friends gave him stories about the paisanos, too, but essentially they became John's creation.

The actual place name of Tortilla Flat was derived from another part of the Peninsula entirely. It came from the Carmel side of the hill, and dated back to the early days of the 1906 earthquake.

At that time a number of well-known bohemian artists and writers from San Francisco took up residence in Carmel, some one hundred miles to the south, and they hoped, outside of the zone of another earthquake like the one that had destroyed the City.

They built a close knit colony along the seashore and planted Monterey pines around their board-and-batten cabins. Many of them were well-known published authors: Sinclair Lewis, George Sterling, Jack London, Mary Austin, Ida M. Tarbell, Fred Bechdolt, Jimmy Hopper, and others who settled there for a short while or permanently.

Because most of these writers were successful enough to afford household help, an obliging group of paisanos—half Mexican, half Carmel Valley Indian—had moved in to supply that help. They built a row of little squatters' shacks, just outside of town, in a wooded area that is now Second Street. The wives of the paisanos came down into town to do daytime housework, and occasionally their more indolent husbands could be prevailed upon to do a bit of gardening or light handiwork.

The writers and other wits of early Carmel had dubbed this row of paisano shacks Tortilla Flat, and the name stuck for many years. Steinbeck liked the name and appropriated it for his story, applying it to another part of the peninsula—the hilly area above the canneries in New Monterey.

This land rises steeply up to Pine Street, where most of the cannery workers lived in small frame houses. Above Pine, in the 1930s, the houses thinned out and the tall pines took over. The ground cover between the trees was mostly wild huckleberry bushes, and the town kids who came up to harvest the berries in coffee cans called it Huckleberry Hill, although there were several other hills on the Peninsula given the same name, probably by other troops of berry stained kids.

Shaky Tom, the old character after whom John had patterned the Pirate, lived in the last little shack at the top

Fred Bechdolt

Boiling Out the Nets — Jackson St. Monterey.   bruce ariss 1936

of our particular Huckleberry Hill, beside an old wooden water tank. The hill actually crested farther on, inside the Presidio, where it was known as Hill 770, which was the military reference to its height above sea level.

I soon discovered that Shaky Tom, or Old Shaky, as the kids called him because of his palsy, wasn't the Pirate's real name either. It was an English name—Lloyd Lytton. He wasn't a paisano, but an eccentric Britisher, not quite right in the head, who kept a dozen mongrel dogs for his closest companions. He called himself "The Poet of the Pines" and wrote doggerel that was occasionally published in the little Pacific Grove weekly newspaper.

Old Man Bishop, who owned the nearby tree nursery on the back highway to Carmel, told me he received a monthly check from "a good family in England" to care for the old man and his dogs. So it seems that Steinbeck's paisano Pirate was actually an English remittance man.

Unlike Steinbeck's Pirate (large, black bearded, slovenly), Shaky Tom was small, clean shaven, and neatly dressed. His white hair was carefully combed. He usually wore a white shirt and pale blue trousers, held up by black suspenders. Like the Pirate, he was followed wherever he walked by his pack of mongrel dogs. Steinbeck said there were six. I counted over ten, more than enough to pull up an extra dog or two, if he got cold at night, as John had described it in one scene in his book.

Like the Pirate, Old Shaky had always been considered a bit loony by his paisano neighbors, ("one of his skull fuses is blowed"), but otherwise quite harmless.

There were two other Tortilla Flat locations that John mentioned to us in passing. One was Charley Shane's house, which belonged to a tippling Irish sign painter, and was located across from the library in Monterey, where the new fire department building now stands. Charley was a happy-go-lucky character. Whenever he painted a sign and had funds, he bought wine for all his friends. Another contributing location was out along the ridge above the college football field. A small, brown skinned paisano called Pilon and some of his friends had built flimsy shelters under the oak trees, where they waxed philosophic over their 29¢ gallon jugs of red wine.

Dick Albee, one of the Lab Group, also recalled going with John in the early 1930s out to Seaside, a little town just north of Monterey, to visit some paisanos who lived out there in the sand dunes.

Perhaps all this has answered the perennial tourist question: Where is Tortilla Flat? The half dozen or more Monterey Peninsula locations were synthesized into one magic, sunny spot by Steinbeck's story telling ability. As a boy, John had been greatly impressed by a gift copy of Malory's *Morte D'Arthur*, and it amused him to write *Tortilla Flat* as though the local Monterey paisanos were the old knights of the Round Table in contemporary dungarees.

I thought Huckleberry Hill, in the days before our art colony developed up there, was closer to Steinbeck's description of Tortilla Flat than any of the other places he mentioned. The location was certainly correct—the hilly pine covered area on the skyline above the canneries. And the scene was also right—unpaved streets, with little paisano shacks half-hidden amongst the trees.

Today most people assume Huckleberry Hill is the location John meant as Tortilla Flat. Not too long ago, a large circulation national magazine ran a color photo, taken from my front gate, of the grape stake fence and the little red studio next door. It was entitled "Tortilla Flat," without any further qualifications.

In 1937 and 1938, the "Okies"—refugees from the dying mid-western Dust Bowl—began arriving in California in their old jalopies. Huckleberry Hill's cheap land and easy terms appealed to them too, and the artists and the Oakies bought lots more or less alternately across the hill. Hobson's choice: Take the next unsold ones in the block, whether you've seen 'em or not.

The Okies immediately cut down all the trees from their lots, rigged them up for firewood, and built their shacks in the center of their clearings, in the manner of their pioneer ancestors. The artists, on the other hand, squeezed their cabins between the trees and then planted more. This gave the area a rather curious "tufted checkerboard" appearance.

Like most artists, I'd always wanted to find a nice old barn and convert it into a studio. I didn't have the money to buy an old barn, but I had unlimited energy, so I helped people tear down old buildings and barns in exchange for the lumber, which I stockpiled. I even saved the second hand nails, in five gallon buckets, to straighten out later as I needed them.

My plan was to build my own barn from recycled

materials, then remodel it afterward into a studio. Land on Huckleberry Hill was the cheapest and most available at the time. Some old guy named Withers had started to lay out the area as a subdivision just before the '29 Crash, and then had given it up. His widow remarried, and decided to liquidate the Hill. They put the lots on sale for only $30-$50 apiece. Ten dollars down, five dollars a month. No interest charges and no questions asked about credit rating. Even my WPA salary of $34.56 a month could meet those requirements.

We started with two lots, soon bought three more, and eventually ended up with fifteen in a group—about half a block in all. At first everyone said I was as crazy as my closest neighbor, the Pirate, to build up there in the woods. No one else would ever live in such a place, they told me. There was no gas or lights, no streets, no sewers, no police, and no fire protection. I had to measure up though the trees with a steel tape from David Avenue, at the foot of the hill, which was the closest piece of surveyed land with a paved street and a corner telephone pole that I could uses as a point of reference.

But at least, I told my artist friends, it was a place you could call your own. Plenty of trees, poison oak, fresh air, and silence. Herds of deer wandered through the brush. Raccoons and squirrels were all over. They said there were bears and skunks, too, but I never saw any. Or smelled any. Artists who lived over in nearby Carmel were always outraged when their landlords raised their rents from $15 in the winter to $25 in the summer, just because it was a tourist trap town. I persuaded some of them to build over on my hill. "We'll start a new artists' colony," I told them. "Better than Carmel."

The paisanos from down the hill, who came up to see what I was doing, thought I was a bit touched, like the Pirate, because I was digging down so deep and using concrete. Most of their places were built on "mud sills"—redwood planks laid on top of the ground. If there was an earthquake the house could bounce around and you could push it back in place afterward. But with such big foundations as those! Who knows what would happen!

One morning when I was working on my studio, John Steinbeck hiked up through the woods to see how I was coming along. He stared up at me where I was perched on the ridge of the unfinished three-story barn. I was working on the gambrel-type roof, which was the broken-shoulder pitch type common to mid-western barns. I hadn't put any siding on the frame yet, or any sheathing on the rafters, and in the mist, the structure looked extremely tall, looming high up amongst the pines.

"What the hell are you building?" John wanted to know. "A dirigible hangar?"

I climbed down, grinning, and we opened a couple of beers I had cooling in a bucket. "It won't look so tall or so big when I put lean-tos all the way around it," I told him.

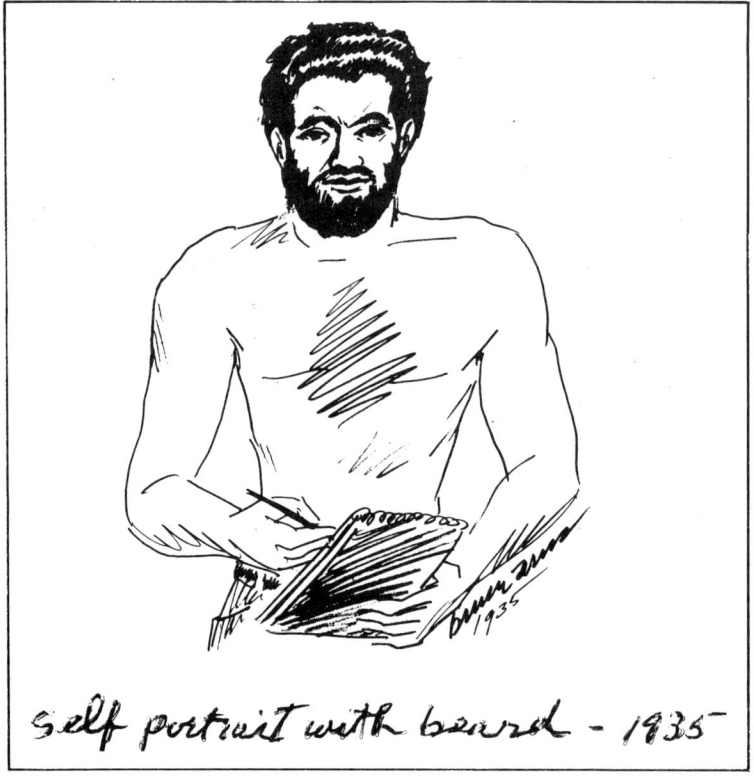

self portrait with beard - 1935

Sea Pride Sardine Cannery Boilers, Monterey

"Jean and I are both string-savers. I've got tons of old used building materials. Jean says I should just build a warehouse with a lean-to kitchen on it. I've salvaged timbers, plumbing, windows, doors, and so on. Trouble is, I don't have much finishing materials. Siding, wallboard, and stuff like that usually gets smashed in any demolition job, and so it's hard to come by. I've picked up some used redwood siding from the old Del Monte Bath House they're tearing down out on the beach. Trouble is it's curved, from the Victorian bay windows. I've got it wet and under weights, trying to straighten it out."

"Fantastic," John grinned. "It's going to be a triumph over architecture!"

"Triumph Over Architecture," I nodded. "A great name for the place! Mind if I adopt it?"

John came up the hill occasionally to check my progress. He was still putting in long hours writing in his little chickenshed garden studio and he needed the walk for his daily exercise. Most of the time he would walk down to Cannery Row to talk to Ed, except in the height of the sardine season when the smell of burning fish was awful. It was overwhelming, almost unbearable. On days and nights when the catches were heavy, the canneries operated around the clock. They worked straight through until all the fish were sealed in their fat oval cans, or squeezed flat of their oil, or burned dry in the giant rotating iron cylinders where they made the fish into fertilizer meal.

This last process was the smelliest of them all. When there was no wind, or a sudden down draught, the coarse yellow smoke from the retorts and chimneys curled along the street, gagging the passersby who hurried along with handkerchiefs held to their noses.

The horrifying aroma in those early days gave rise to a very popular description of the Monterey Peninsula's three small cities: the town full of tourists, art galleries, and gift shops was Carmel-by-the-Sea, the town full of churches and quaint Victorian cottages was Pacific-Grove-by-God, and the sardine packing town was Monterey-by-the-Smell.

Since it was a time of little money and fewer jobs, this malodorous seasonal prosperity actually was welcomed.

Ten million dollars worth of fish went through the pipeline of the local economy. Itinerant workers, who harvested crops in the off-season, swelled the local population, looking for work. The transients arrived in old jalopy buses, or riding the freights, and found what lodging they could. Their polyglot voices filled the air with shouts and noisy conversations. The greasy-spoon workers' restaurants were open all night. The whorehouses, of which there were at least six "official" ones, did a fine, bouncing business.

The battered old cars of workers vied for parking spaces with big trailer trucks along the six-block long waterfront street. Little kids slept on the seats of some of the cars at night, while parents worked inside. I remember seeing mothers on their breaks, dressed in their heavy sweatshirts, overalls, and high rubber boots, rushing out to check on their kids, or to give the youngest ones a quick breast to keep them quiet and sleepy.

Over it all was the thump and clank of heavy machinery, the hiss of steam, the sound of motors, the hoarse whistles from the boats and canneries. Each cannery had its own distinctive pattern of toots and shrills to alert their workers of a catch coming in. One long, one short, or one long and three shorts, or whatever, would blast out across the sky. Then down the hill and along the streets came the workers, their floppy boots making a sloshing noise on the pavement as they hurried to their appointed places at the fish-cutting chains.

Fish & Game check-up Monterey Harbor 1936

Ed Ricketts' biological business at the Lab was mainly preserving marine shore-life specimens. Most of the collecting of these specimens he did himself in the nearby coastal tidepools, although he was often aided by his large coterie of friends, mostly unemployed young artists and writers, who were attracted to his gentle and thoughtful manner and the coffee-house conviviality of his waterfront laboratory. It had become a sort of Depression day social club, and Ed was probably what would now be called its guru.

He could nearly always dig up enough cheese, crackers, and red wine, mix them with some of his provocative ideas, and then toss them into a casual gathering of his bohemian friends. The resulting spirited argument was enough to entertain him and his friends for the rest of the day, through the evening, and often long into the night.

Ed was a compact, middle-sized, and middle-aged man with a fair complexion and a shock of reddish-brown hair. He had large, expressive brown eyes that crinkled when he smiled. He was clean-shaven in those days and didn't grow his celebrated beard until after the Lab burned down, late in 1936, sometime after we returned from the Baja trip.

John Steinbeck called it a "Triumph Over Architecture"

Along the Row, his learned vocabulary and professional air had earned him his popular nickname of "Doc." Little kids with skinned knees actually believed he was a doctor, and came to him to have their wounds disinfected and bandaged. So did many of the bums and some of the hard-up cannery workers. Even the whores from Flora's Lone Star Restaurant across the street would stop in after a hard night, for a little first aid, or perhaps a morning cup of coffee and some fatherly consolation and advice.

His close friends tried to remember to call him Ed. If they slipped and called him Doc, as most people did, he was so painstakingly honest that he'd launch into an automatic denial of having a doctor's degree. Or any degree, for that matter. Just as his friend Steinbeck had done at Stanford, Ed had attended, but never graduated from, the University of Chicago. Ed had been a biology student there in the early 1920s. He picked up enough knowledge and interest in those short years to go at his life's work on his own. Like many widely read and largely self-educated people, he was probably better off for having skipped a lot of the deadly academic nonsense considered necessary for a degree.

Ed was what the Spanish call *Muy Simpatico*. Almost instinctively he was aware of people's problems, often before they were themselves. Probably his most endearing

"Monterey by the Smell"
IN THE REDUCTION PLANTS
the Fertilizer Mill was the BIG offender
1937

virtue was that he knew how to listen. This ability, more of a feminine than a masculine trait, was one that John Steinbeck envied in his friend, but didn't have in his own macho makeup. John talked *at* people instead of *with* them.

Ed liked women as people, as adults, treating them as equals long before feminine consciousness was awakened. His attitude was so unusual then, that Ed often found himself the center of a group of instinctively intelligent women talking to him on a high intellectual level. John, on the other hand, didn't really like women, according to Jean. I felt he was afraid of them, or didn't trust them. It amused him to argue with them, or tease them, or intimidate them, or outrage them with his occasionally too frank and brutal yarns. Fundamentally, we thought he considered women as the enemy, or only in the light of fancied conquests, as sex objects, as they do nowadays.

John envied Ed's easy avuncular approach with girls, but he didn't understand it. Instead, he projected his own attitudes on to those of his friend. Ed's reputation as a "womanizer" was one largely manufactured by John. His memorial essay "About Ed Ricketts" antagonized Ed's family and friends, who felt it was patronizing, negative, and demeaning. They felt it was as if Boswell had written "The Life of Johnson" to prove that Dr. Johnson was a minor influence on his, Boswell's, life.

John's depiction of Ed as a fire-breathing Casanova was ridiculous, of course, but it made good copy. His misrepresentation of Ed has been carried on to this day by others with the same envious partiality for such salacious yarns.

This is not to say that Ed was a prude or celibate. He'd been separated from his wife, Nan, by whom he had three handsome children, for a number of years, and he considered himself an available bachelor. He had a few discreet liaisons and, although his divorce was never finished, he lived as man and wife at the Lab with a beautiful girl, Toni Siexas Jackson, for a number of years.

Toni and Ed broke up when she fell in love with another marine biologist, an exchange student at the nearby Hopkins Institute, whom she married when they moved to Israel. Ed subsequently married Alice Ricketts, who apparently was unaware that their marriage was not legal until after Ed was killed in the 1948 train accident.

I don't think Ed was aware of it either. If an "absent-minded professor" can drive in front of an express train that's been crossing in front of his door every evening at the same time for twenty years, it's not impossible that he'd forgotten he hadn't signed a final divorce decree some fifteen years previously.

Ed was actually a gentleman of the old school; quiet, considerate, and overly concerned for other people's feelings. Again, this is not to say that he was a milktoast, or that his good nature was endless. Once in a while, when he'd been imposed upon too much, it was said he exploded in a terrible temper tantrum. The only time I remember Ed losing his temper happened after he grew his beard, about 1937. Ed asked Jean and me to keep him company one day while he drove to his Monterey post office box. Jean and I climbed with him into the wide front seat of his old Packard limousine.

Old Monterey, like Boston, was purportedly laid out by cows, and to get to the post office, zig-zagging around blocks was necessary. At one intersection, Jefferson and Main (Now Calle Principal) Ed almost had a fender-bender with a young Sicillian fisherman in an old Ford sedan.

FISH CUTTING CHAINS

John's 11½ St Cottage
Pacific Grove

Both cars screeched to a halt within inches of each other.

"Hey! Ya goddamn old goat," the fisherman roared. "Didn't ya see that stop sign?"

"No, I didn't," Ed yelled back, "and I don't believe there is one!"

The fisherman backed his car around, jammed it in gear, and dashed off, cursing. Ed was so furious he drove around the block at breakneck speed to check for a stop sign. There was none. Then he sped recklessly after the distant Ford.

"For God's sake, take it easy, Ed," Jean entreated. "Do you want to get us all killed over a stupid shouting match?"

Ed caught up with the sedan on Carmel Hill and drove his big Packard in front of it, forcing it off the road. Then he dashed out and confronted the fisherman.

"There was no stop sign there! I don't like the way you yelled at me, and I want an apology!"

The young man got out of the car. I opened the car door on my side, ready to get out in case Ed needed help, but fortunately, the young fellow was smaller than Ed and thoroughly intimidated by Ed's righteous wrath. He apologized contritely. Ed stalked to the car and we drove back down to the post office.

Jean was not amused. She scolded Ed for his ridiculous escapade. "You could have had your face punched in if he'd been a big tough," she told him.

"Someone said you had a temper," I said. "But that's the first time I ever saw an example of it. What did you plan to do? Beat that guy up if he didn't apologize? Have you ever had any training in protecting yourself in a fist fight?"

"No, I haven't," Ed admitted. "And I was too angry to worry about it."

I was a heavyweight boxer in college and had a fine set of 16-ounce training gloves. I made a few dollars now and then giving boxing lessons to Pebble Beach kids, and at the moment I was teaching the fundamentals to Ed's eager twelve year old son, Ed, Junior.

"You'd better sit in with Little Ed and me this afternoon," I suggested. "Next time you lose your temper you might not be so lucky."

Ed agreed and the three of us went through the steps of learning a good left jab and a solid right cross, the two punches, I felt, were all that were needed in an average encounter. Ed was surprisingly quick at learning the punches, and how to crouch under a counter-blow. We were stepping around noisily, upstairs in the Lab, when John walked in. I'd heard he had been a boxer at Stanford so I asked him if he wanted to go a few rounds with me.

"Hell no," John said darkly, "I'm not a boxer, I'm a fighter! When I get going, I don't stop. I'm afraid I might kill somebody."

I grinned but didn't say anything. I'd heard that line before and accepted it for what it was—the macho's smokescreen.

John had a positively proprietary attitude toward Ed. He felt he had known him longer than any of the rest of us had, which was probably true. There were several dozen of Ed's friends of all ages who wandered in and out of the Lab. There was usually a group of six or eight at a time there, but John somehow always assumed he had a prior right. When he barged in, he immediately singled Ed out, and crossed to sit by Ed's chair. If all the other seats around him were filled, John would sit on the floor by his feet.

After a long writing session in the little shack in his garden, John would walk the six or eight blocks down to the Lab to use Ed as a sounding board and read aloud his day's work. We noted with amusement that many of John's ideas were actually Ed's, transposed into literary language and played back to him. Ed always listened patiently, nodding his head and making occasional quiet suggestions.

We also noted that John had difficulty suppressing his irritation when Ed diverted his attention to someone else. An example that stands out in my memory was one of those rare nights when only Ed, John, Jean, and myself happened to be in the Lab. It was the off-canning season and the Row was deserted. Flora, the Madame from the House across the street, probably seeing us through the open windows, sent her skinny handyman over to invite us all to see a lesbian show. He said two of her girls were planning to put one on, to liven up an otherwise dull evening.

Ed decided arbitrarily that he and John would go, but Jean and I should stay in the Lab, and because we were so young and such newlyweds, we wouldn't appreciate that sort of exhibition anyway.

"Ed's right," John put in. He was just as arbitrary about it. "You two are always sitting around holding hands, or with your arms around each other's necks. It's disgusting. And you never fight or argue the way Carol and I do. I really can't believe that's true love, when you don't even argue."

John and Carol were famous for their battles both in public and private. Russ Cummings, the young Pacific Grove photographer (who took the color pictures of Ed's marine specimens for *Between Pacific Tides*) had a small makeshift darkroom against the back of the little house the Steinbecks rented on Second Street. Whenever Russ was in the darkroom and the Steinbecks were yelling and throwing things next door, he said he had to hold the bottles on his shelves to keep them from bouncing off.

"The only way you can tell true love is when two people are squaring off to break each other's noses," John insisted pompously.

"That's ridiculous, John," Jean said. "You're just

Ed without beard c. 1935

trying to change the subject. I want to go to the lesbian show. I've never seen one."

"No, I don't think you should," Ed told her. "Listen, I'm old enough to be your father. Just take my advice for once."

Ed liked to consider himself the senior citizen of the group. He was still barely forty, but he was roughly five years older than John, fifteen years older than I, and twenty years older than Jean, who was still in her late teens.

I didn't want Jean to go, either, and said so. "I bet Flora couldn't see from across the street that you're a girl. You're wearing jeans and a man's shirt and have a boyish bob.

She probably thought you were just another prospective male customer."

"That's nonsense, Bruce! If it's a real lesbian show, how do you know? Maybe Flora's putting it on just for me, and not for you men at all!"

The three of us grinned indulgently. Jean was marvelous at such convoluted logic. She anticipated the women's rights movement by decades. She carried on, protesting dramatically that simply because she was a poor under-aged girl, she was being blatantly discriminated against in a domineering masculine world.

"Believe me, Jean!" Ed was amused by her histrionics, but still insisted he was right. "It's not for you."

"Oh, Ed! You make me sick!" I knew Jean was only pretending to be furiously angry, but I don't think the other two did. She opened up on Ed first. "Just because you're so old you can sit around on their mornings after and hold those poor girls' hands—and feed them tea and cookies and fatherly advice—you think you can tell me what I can or can't do? Hah! I know you! Everyone says you're the patron saint of that whorehouse across the street, but if you're a patron, how can you be a saint? You're probably just another dirty old man, and you don't want me to find out what you do when you go over there!"

"Hey, come on! Take it easy," John was trying to be placating, but Jean turned on him with equal ferocity.

"And as for you, John, you big idiot! Your definition of true love being a dog and cat fight doesn't define my relationship with Bruce, only yours with Carol. If you'd give her a little more attention and love now and then, you wouldn't have to sneak across the street to see how other people do it!"

The three of us were laughing helplessly at Jean's outbursts, but her fireworks hadn't changed our minds. I sat on her while Ed and John escaped across to Flora's. After they left I let Jean up. She flounced over to Ed's massive phonograph. It was one that his friend, Pol Verbeck, the Belgian electrical wizard, had custom-built for him. She put on one of Ed's recordings of early Gregorian chants.

"I ought to turn this thing up full volume and blast them out of there with this good old church music," she said darkly.

"You wouldn't," I laughed.

"No, of course not! But I can just imagine how Ed would feel. Those lesbians squirming away to his favorite religious music!"

"You didn't really want to see a cheap show like that. And you were pretty hard on those two guys, the way you told them off."

"You're right. I guess I didn't really want to go. I just like to needle Ed and John. I love to see how outraged they can look. The hypocrites! I bet they're not looking outraged over there now, when those two girls are probably putting on a stupid act against their wills, and against their better judgment."

In half an hour Ed and John came back and rejoined us. They looked non-committal and wouldn't tell us anything about Flora's show.

"Well, did you get your kicks?" Jean demanded.

"Hell, no," John said. "It was a fake, a put-on."

"It was spoor-ious," Ed added, meaning spurious. It was one of his favorite words, but one which he invariably mispronounced. "Just two poor little prostitutes in a dumb show. Their hearts weren't in it. It was obvious to me they weren't really lesbians."

"You know *everything*, don't you Ed?" Jean said pointedly, as usual, getting the last word in any debate.

Annually, for his marine biology business, Ed collected specimens during the low spring tides, either up or down the Pacific Coast. In 1936 he told us he was planning to drive south to Mexico. He then asked John, Jean, and myself if we wanted to go along and help out.

Without hesitation Jean and I agreed. I still had a sixteen foot wide WPA mural to finish, but I couldn't go back to work on it until after the end of the month, when the preliminary drawings and the full-scale cartoon had been okayed by a citizen's committee consisting of Nellie Montague, the Carmel art gallery curator, Una Jeffers, the poet's wife, and Sumner Greene, the architect. I was just marking time, so it was a fine opportunity for me to get away.

John wanted to go too, and he said it couldn't have come at a better time for him, either. He was between novels and, because his work never seemed to get any easier for him, he needed a vacation. He was burned out from too many hours of creative writing. He had just received the galley proofs of his latest book, but he could check them over at his leisure while on the trip, as long as he didn't have to drive. He didn't like to drive that big old car of Ed's. Carol was out of town anyway, supervising the construction of their new house in Los Gatos.

Carol had almost completed a year's venture, a brand new country house on two acres of land outside the little town of Los Gatos, in the Santa Cruz Mountains. She had designed it and was financing it from the money coming in mostly from the sales of *Tortilla Flat* and some from John's latest book, *In Dubious Battle*, a powerful strike novel that was creating a nationwide controversy. Although its sales were not as phenomenal as the earlier

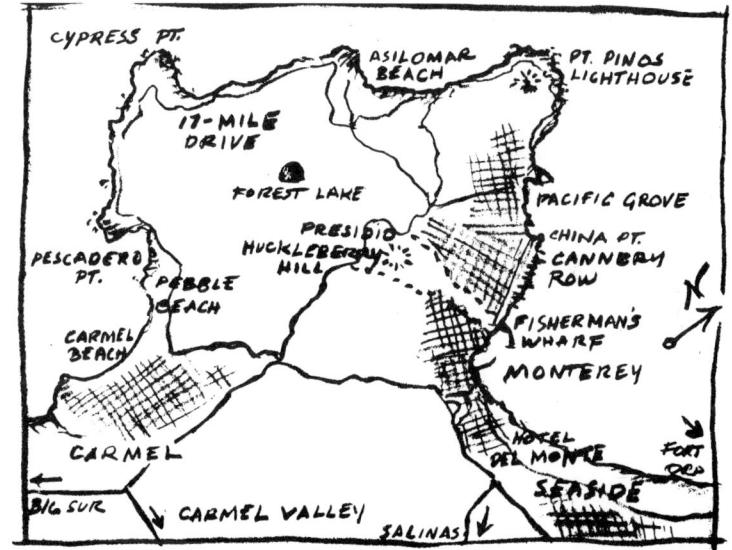

A MAP OF MONTEREY PENINSULA—"THE BEAR'S HEAD"

Wreck of the New Cravello, 9/17/36 Point Pinos

humorous novel, they felt they could afford to build at last.

John said they were justified in spending the money from *Tortilla Flat* to build their new place, since all his irritating notoriety had resulted from its success—a success that was making escape from his public a downright necessity. He still wrote in his Pacific Grove garden shed, and in an effort to protect his privacy he tacked a small sign on the gate, which read, as I remember:

I am a working writer. Please do not interrupt me between 9:30 a.m. and 4:30 p.m.

Thank you—J. Steinbeck.

Jean and I read it thoughtfully one beautiful afternoon on our way down to the Lab to discuss the Mexican trip with Ed. We thought he might want to go down with us, but since it was only 2 o'clock, we went on without bothering him.

"Hey, wait up for Christ's sake!" John came pounding down the street after us. "You guys have the longest legs! No wonder you like to walk so much! Why didn't you come in?"

"We read your note."

"Oh, that! That thing's no good. I've got to take it down. I put it up last week to keep strangers out, but they barge right in anyway. Only my friends, the ones I want to see, pay any attention to it!"

John walked with us along the S.P. tracks on China Point, past the Boatworks, to the Lab. He had developed a slight limp and was envying our long strides. He said he was suffering occasionally from attacks of sciatica in his right leg. He thought it had developed from sitting in one position too long while he wrote. He'd just bought enough diamond-pointed red roll-roofing to redo his house, but he wasn't up to it. Probably take two men. He'd be willing to pay me if I wanted to tackle it. He could actually afford to pay, nowadays. What did I think?

"Sure," I said. "Why not? Maybe Ellwood Graham would work with me when we come back from Mexico. He's very handy with tools."

We strolled on down along China Point toward the Lab. The bay breeze was sharp with the good smell of salt and seaweed. John was right about our love of walking. In the

"Derelict"

two years of our honeymooning Jean and I had crisscrossed almost daily back and forth over the Peninsula. We often walked all day, from dawn to sunset.

The Monterey Peninsula was, and still is, a marvelous hiking place. It's surprisingly small, roughly circular, and very heavily wooded. From the tip of Huckleberry

Hill, looking only five miles in every direction, you can see its irregular coastline sweep all the way around from Monterey to the east to Carmel to the south. From a high-flying plane it looks like a bear's head jutting out into the sea. Carmel is on the back of its neck, the two ears are at Pescadero Point in Pebble Beach and at Cypress Point. To the north, its nose supports a sparkling lighthouse at Point Piños. Pacific Grove is in the bear's mouth, Cannery Row lies under its jaw, and Monterey, the largest of the three towns, spreads out along its throat and chest. The bear's head even has a bright blue eye in just the right place, Forest Lake, the large water company reservoir "Inside the Property."

FISH WEIGHING TOWER

For six months in 1878, Robert Louis Stevenson hiked over the Peninsula, then was said to have used it as his model for *Treasure Island*. Movie companies were constantly filming on it. Hollywood used its idyllic location backgrounds to represent almost every country in the world.

Steinbeck also used the Monterey area as a whimsical backdrop for his three most popular works of humorous fiction, *Tortilla Flat*, and later, *Cannery Row* and *Sweet Thursday*. The first time he used Ed and his Cannery Row laboratory for a setting was in his short story *The Snake*, which he wrote shortly after we met him.

There's always speculation these days about how much real life contributed to Steinbeck's fiction. He frequently said this particular snake yarn was based on an actual occurrence. I think it was built on three separate incidents, which John later wove into one story. The first incident, which inspired the opening sequence, happened in the spring of 1935.

John and I were sitting in the Lab early one foggy morning, talking idly, when we heard the sound of determined footsteps on the outside stairway, followed by a moment of silence, and then a crisp knock on the door. Ed was working at his rolltop desk in the entry alcove. He groaned and got up to answer it. He hated doing secretarial work and his desk was always a mess. Carol, Jean, Tal Lovejoy, or Marge Lloyd would try to make some sense out of his business papers now and then, stacking his open and unopened mail in separate piles, but he'd come in looking for something, and in a few seconds it would be messed up again. When he did get at his work, someone was always interrupting him. He took the few steps to the door and opened it reluctantly. John and I, in the other room, stopped talking and turned to see who it was. It had to be a stranger. The door was never locked and everyone else barged right in.

"Are you Mr. Ricketts?" A middle-aged spinsterish-looking woman, in an ankle-length tweedy skirt and matching suit-jacket, stood on the stoop. She had grayish nondescript hair, cut in a long straight bob, with an out of style 1920s cloche hat clamped over it. She looked like a math teacher or a dean from an eastern girls' college.

"Yes, I am." Out of instinctive politeness Ed removed the baseball cap he wore when he worked, which kept his hair from falling over his eyes. Ed was clean-shaven in those days, as was John, and I was the only one with a beard.

"May I come in?"

"Yes, of course." Ed cleared his throat. "But I'm awfully busy. What is it you want?"

The woman stepped inside, glanced hesitantly at John and me, then voiced a strange request. "I hear you keep snakes. I want to buy a snake."

Ed looked uncomfortable. "Well, I don't really sell snakes. I keep them for experimental purposes."

"Oh, don't misunderstand me!" The woman hurried on in a low, rapid voice. "I wouldn't take the snake away. I'd leave it here. You could do whatever you need to do with it. I mean, I just want to feed it and own it. It's just that, well, you see, I'd like to have a snake of my own."

In the other room, which opened directly into the entry alcove, John and I were pretending to read magazines. We didn't dare look at each other for fear we'd burst out laughing. The poor woman's request had such obvious Freudian overtones we found it unbelievably naive and hilarious. We couldn't allow ourselves to giggle, or even have a coughing fit, because we were afraid she might suddenly realize the implications. We knew if she did, she'd probably die of embarrassment.

"May I see the snakes now?" she persisted.

"Yes, I suppose so." Ed sounded dubious, but was obviously at a loss for excuses. "I guess you can—if you'll come this way."

Ed led her into the back room where he kept the cages of rattlesnakes. In the outer room John and I doubled over in silent laughter.

"Can you believe it?" John whispered. "Poor Ed! He doesn't know how to handle this one!"

"Incredible!" I chortled. "And she's such a proper and puritanical looking old gal."

Purse Seine Net Menders, Old Fisherman's Wharf 1983

We managed to regain our composure before they returned. Ed was being patient and polite but was still firmly against her proposal. "I'm sorry, but I couldn't possibly sell, or even rent, a rattlesnake. It would be dangerous and, um, unprofessional."

The woman seemed very disappointed about it as he ushered her out the door. Ed turned to join us in silent laughter.

"There's one for the book," he told John.

That was all there was to the encounter, but it was obvious that it had inspired John's snake story. Since it was incomplete, he had rounded it out with several other incidents to make it into what is now considered to be a work of short story art.

Toby Street, one of John's oldest and best friends, who had been his roommate at Stanford, remembered a pretty dancer who visited the Lab one day. She watched Ed feed them their dinner of white rats with breathless excitement. Toby felt this incident had inspired the short story. John's first wife, Carol, also remembered Ed feeding the white rats to the rattlesnakes in their three cages in the front windows of the Lab.

"I told John and he wrote *The Snake* on the strength of it," she recalled.

The Lab was heated by an old gas floor furnace that Ed turned on with a key. The pilot was sparked by two Model T Ford coils, rigged up by Pol Verbeck, which made a buzzing sound like a rattlesnake before the gas ignited. This was enough warning to awaken Ed's three-foot long pet king snake, who slept in the bottom of the furnace. It would come pouring up out of the floor register grating just in time to keep from getting singed. Ed was used to this phenomenon, and kept right on talking without missing a beat, but it was disconcerting to guests or strangers. In particular, there was one memorable occasion. Ed had leaned over to turn on the floor furnace, just after serving a cup of hot tea to Jean's Daughters of the American Revolution grandmother, on that very dignified lady's first and last visit to the Lab.

The only professional help Ed ever received with his bookkeeping problems happened more or less by accident. One day he answered a knock at his door to discover two sombre looking men in business suits and snap-brim hats. At first glance he thought they were a couple of Mormons inquiring about the condition of his soul, but they weren't. They were two Feds from the Bureau of Alcohol, Tobacco, and Firearms, and they were interested in a more worldly topic.

Their division had been sending Ed threatening letters for six months, none of which he answered. The two Feds grimly demanded he tell them what he was doing with all the alcohol he'd been purchasing. Apparently, his address on Cannery Row—in the heart of the red light district—combined with the fact that he ignored their correspondence, had led them to believe he was operating

a bootlegging establishment.

Ed invited them in, gave them a quick tour of the Lab, then took them downstairs to show them he was only using the alcohol to preserve specimens. After a bit, they came back upstairs, grinning and in a much friendlier mood. Ed proceeded to search through the six-inch layer of correspondence on his roll-top desk. He finally located all the letters they had sent, still unopened. The two Feds, charmed by his absent-minded professor's manner, took off their coats and hats, and spent several days opening his correspondence and trying to set up a bookkeeping system for him.

While all this was going on, Ed went back to work in the basement. His business was essentially a one-man operation. Their interruption had put him behind schedule, but he came up, occasionally, to see how they were doing, and to serve them cups of hot tea, lightly spiked with rum.

John was a natural story teller. He was at his best around a fire at the beach where he was humorous, ribald, lusty, devilishly droll, sarcastic, or full of his own chortling laughter. But privately, he was a dedicated student of literature. He liked to discuss his theories of writing. Unhappily, with his increasing notoriety I was finding it more and more difficult to isolate him for a one-on-one discussion of literature.

About the time he'd get his feet up, relax, and start talking, some newcomer would break in to ask him the same stupid questions he'd answered hundreds of times before. In a few moments he'd give up. With a cornered-animal look, he'd make a hasty excuse and slip out the door.

One day John and I walked over to see Gus Gay in his studio in the Old Stevenson House in Monterey. Gus was one of our favorite characters. August Pierre François Gay, or Gus for short, was a loveable curmudgeon, an old French painter, who looked very much like Albert Einstein. He had the same nimbus crown of gray hair, smoked a briar pipe, wore seedy clothes and tennis shoes and, in general, was a great pleasure to be around.

Gus was as much a natural painter as John was a natural story teller. Perhaps more so because, unlike John, he didn't bother with any theories, either before or after he created a work of art. He'd simply start painting in the lower left-hand corner of a canvas and keep working clockwise around the top until he came down to the bottom right-hand corner, where he'd sign his name, A. F. Gay. I could swear he didn't have the slightest idea where he was going—no preliminary sketches or charcoal outlines—he just painted. Yet his pictures were always little jewel-like masterpieces when he finished.

Gus told us he had come to America as a lad of thirteen and had a lot of amusing experiences learning English and working at odd jobs in San Francisco before and after World War I. He moved to Monterey "because Monterey reminds me of Gap," his native village in the south of France.

I talked about my student days painting in Berkeley and being influenced by Diego Rivera and Chiura Obata. John told about his early experiences in Salinas and later, at Stanford. It was a friendly, low-key conversation and John was obviously enjoying it.

John and I sat on the sunny wooden bench with Gus in his French peasant's vegetable garden and relaxed. We were without a care in the world. We talked quietly away for a good part of the afternoon.

Unfortunately, the Stevenson House was on the tourists' route, and a group of old ladies recognized John as they passed by. They flocked around him chattering like chickens. One of them had met him once at a cocktail party, didn't he remember?

John arose from his seat with a look of pure panic. He dug a pair of dark glasses out of his shirt pocket, put them

The Boatworks on China Point 1935

Amcanco gangpress

on, then ducked away through the garden, running in a crouch out the gate.

The chickens stood with their mouths open for a moment, then fluttered off. Gus went away grumbling to himself, and disappeared back into his adobe-walled studio to work. I wandered out to the street looking for John. He was leaning against Gus' old shovel-nosed Franklin sedan, which looked exactly like one of the World War I French taxis that saved Paris. John's dark glasses were still perched on his nose. It occurred to me that he must secretly be enjoying all this attention he was getting, perhaps because of his years of rejection slips, when he feared he'd never be recognized.

"That was crazy," I told him. "What was the point of the sunglasses after they already knew who you were?"

"Bruce, you don't know how miserable things have been for me lately." He took off the glasses and put them back in his shirt pocket. "Oh, sure! I know those old girls didn't mean any harm. So I guess I'm getting paranoid. But since the publication of *In Dubious Battle* I've been the butt of all kinds of criticism. Left and right. It comes from both extremes of the political spectrum. These days, I don't really know whether some idiot might actually be trying to take a shot at me or not! I'm glad we're leaving for Mexico tomorrow, so I can relax."

I looked at him for a moment, wondering about his rationality lately. He seemed so erratic, so obsessed by the idea of getting away all the time—of going on a trip. Escaping. He sounded like he was abandoning the ship before it went down in a high sea. I shook my head, wondering about John and his apparent compulsion to get away from it all.

Going on a trip. That phrase today has come to mean a fugue from reality, usually through drugs. But then, John's manic fans and followers seemed to be on a trip too—on a compulsion to pester the poor guy out of his skull. It's hard to believe the ridiculous things people were saying about him then, and it was to get much worse later. He once told me some nutty girl he'd scarcely met was claiming he was the father of her baby.

People's behavior around him was becoming bizarre all right, but I found it difficult to take too seriously. I tried to tell him he should just laugh off such nonsense. Ignore it.

"Easy for you," John said lugubriously. "It's not your ox being gored!"

"You think you've got it tough," I said. "Hell, just think what happened to Charley Lindbergh. Drove the poor guy half crazy, wherever he went."

I said all this kind of fuss was probably a form of American madness. Perhaps all our celebrity-chasing was some sort of instinct of counter-democracy, some recrudescent desire to worship royalty again, related to the strange urge that drives wealthy American heiresses to marry worthless European noblemen just for their titles. We discussed it idly. Perhaps the average person, with his average crushed ego, may unconsciously try to identify with imaginary heroes, or attempt to associate with outstanding successful persons such as writers or movie stars. And perhaps the "gilded trappings of state," as in English royal parades, are purposefully created to instil subservient feelings in the populace? In order to insure the self-perpetuation of fundamentally shaky regimes? These speculations were a bit aimless, we decided, but interesting just as speculations.

Of late, I'd felt John had developed an almost superstitious reaction. He seemed to be looking fearfully over his shoulder, expecting God knows what. I agreed with him—the trip to Baja would do him good. We headed back to Cannery Row to see how Ed was doing with the scientific gear he was stowing in his old Packard limousine.

I wondered also if some of John's recent uneasiness could have been traced to the increasingly menacing international situation. He, like most other socially conscious Americans of the period, was getting more and more jumpy at the prospect of another world war. Most of us remembered the First World War and were sweating over the current neutrality problems that might embroil us in a second one.

Far left and far right politics were polarizing on the home front, too, and with his recent strike novel John apparently had opened out his chest to arrows from both extremes. These opposite attacks reassured him only in that it made him feel he must have told it pretty much the way it was.

In retrospect, I find it remarkable how well Steinbeck's books expressed the spirit of his time, in particular, the Depression Decade of the 30s. It was a period of small disasters and large melodramas that lasted from the Stock Market Crash of '29 until the outbreak of the European War, ten years later. It was John's most creative period, and one in which I felt very fortunate to have known him.

From the beginning of the Depression until his death in 1968, over a period of forty years, he published almost thirty books.

His books were generally greeted with disdain by professional and academic critics, although he reached an enthusiastic reading audience around the world. His novels were translated into many languages, and his popularity was unequalled in the Scandinavian countries, in Japan, and in Russia. In the latter country, in the 1960s, his bellicose attitude about Vietnam alienated the Kremlin, but the Russian people still loved his work.

CAL-PACK SEALING MACHINES

All the old cars in Baja seemed to be battered refugees discarded from Southern Californian used car lots. This one was a 1922 Studebaker touring car with demountable rims. John Steinbeck counted nine kids waiting

SECTION II

TRAVELS WITH STEINBECK

ON THE MORNING we set out on the Mexican trip, Jean and I stopped by before sunrise at John's Eleventh Street cottage. We'd agreed the night before to pick him up. There was a light on in the house but the entryway through his side garden was as black as a mine shaft. We stumbled along, trying to keep our footing on the damp stepping stones. I tapped on the glass of his side door.

"Come on in!" John yelled cheerfully, over the brisk barking of his full grown Setter pup, Toby, named after John's good friend, Toby Street. John was dressed in his usual cord trousers, blue work shirt, and heavy workman's shoes. His sheepskin coat was draped over his blanket roll, just inside the door.

"How about a cup of coffee before we hit the road?" John grinned. He seemed to be in a very cheerful mood for so early in the morning.

"Sounds great," Jean replied, slipping out of her leather jacket. "I'm still half asleep."

The coffee smelled marvelous and we sipped carefully at the mugs of steaming black liquid that John offered us. He always ground his own bulk coffee beans (at ten cents a pound) in the big red wheeled antique coffee mill that stood on his kitchen sinkboard. As we came in, we noticed two men, beyond him in the living room, finishing up their coffee and getting ready to leave. They were putting on their workingmen's coats and cloth caps. They were quiet and tense, so much alike in size that at first glance I thought they might be twins. John ushered them out without introducing them to us.

They slung their roped-up blanket rolls over their shoulders, shook hands with John, said a few quiet words, and left. They obviously had stayed overnight, and I presumed they were a pair of union organizers—very likely the ones who helped him research *In Dubious Battle*, his latest published novel about the agricultural strikes. John had also mentioned writing something soon, for a San Francisco newspaper, about the miserable conditions of California's farm laborers and their families in the inland valleys.

"This crazy mutt of a dog!" John apparently was avoiding any discussion of the two men by ruffling Toby's long black ears and changing the subject. "Month or so ago, I was just finishing my new novel. I was lying over there on the rug, working all night. Wrote the last page about dawn and crawled off to bed. When I got up late the next morning, damned if I hadn't left my work on the floor and Toby, here, had chewed it to a pulp."

"How awful," Jean said. "What did you do?"

"I would have kicked him into the middle of next week," I said in disgust.

"No. Hell no. I didn't say a word." John chuckled indulgently, massaging the big dog's shoulders. "I just took out another one of my dad's old black ledgers—just like the one that Toby chewed up—and went back to work. Wrote it all over again in longhand. Turned out much better, too. This pooch has excellent critical taste. He instantly recognized my first draft as being quite tasteless, if not indigestible."

Marge Lloyd, one of our Lab Group, informed me some years later that John had given her an entirely different account of this incident, immediately after it had happened. She said John told her he had been so furious that he scolded and punished his dog severely. Good old unreliable John! He loved to change his stories, almost every time he retold them. He enhanced his yarns, I'm sure, at the moment, but I wonder how much he confused the record for Steinbeck scholars later on.

Still chuckling, John crossed over to the big bookcase which was built into a series of arches across the front of the house. The arches had originally supported the overhang of an open front porch, before they were filled in and incorporated into the living room. He pulled down a black ledger from the lower left shelf. It had a fat flattened roll of white galley sheets stuffed between its covers. It was the re-written manuscript he'd mentioned, plus the new proofs of it from his publisher.

"Well, you better keep those things away from your four footed editor," I told him as I picked up his blanket roll and sheepskin. "Everybody ready to move?"

"In a minute," John said. He measured out a week's supply of dry dog food into a sack to take along with us, and fastened the chain leash on Toby's collar. Jean rinsed the coffee cups in the kitchen sink. John snapped off the lights and closed the door behind us as we stumbled back out through the dark garden and climbed into the car. I started the motor, turned on the lights, and we chugged on down to Cannery Row.

Ed's big Packard limousine, with its motor idling, was standing at the curb in front of the darkened Lab. Everything seemed ready to go. Ed had wired a wooden pickup box to the trunk rack on the rear of the vehicle. The box was about five feet across and added another three or four feet to the length of a car that was already overly long. The box was packed with Ed's collecting gear—metal trays, buckets, hip boots, Coleman lanterns, and a dozen shiny new five gallon square tins that were marked either GAS, H2O, or HCHO—the last being formaldehyde, I guessed.

Ed was in the process of covering the tins with a black tarp and roping them down when we pulled up alongside in the Dodge. He waved us a cordial good morning. When he smiled his eyes almost closed shut, I noticed.

"I scrounged these beautiful tins from a foreman in one of the canneries who's a friend of mine," he told us. "They put sardine oil in them, but these have never been used. Did you know that African natives consider these tins one of the white man's greatest inventions and prize them very highly? I'm using these for formaldehyde for the specimens, gasoline for the car, and the water's for us. Where we're going, below the border, gas is hard to find and

not much good. And drinking water's worse. Dysentery is bad enough, but amoebic dysentery is for life. Incurable."

I backed my old Dodge into the basement garage of the Lab and closed the sliding door around it. Ed climbed in behind the wheel and gunned the motor of the big Packard. Jean got in beside him, and John, Toby, and I settled into the roomy back seat section. Ed put the big car in gear and we started slowly off down the Row.

The Packard was an enormous eight cylinder-in-line automobile, chauffeur driven style, with the front and back sections separated by a vertical crank-down window. The car was black, shiny, had lots of chrome, and sported two huge spare tires in the front fender wells. It had been a great luxury car in its day. Ed had bought it from a bankrupt Pebble Beach estate. It had fine black leather upholstery in front and mohair in back, with cut glass vases for flowers and even a telephone, with a buzzer, that Jean and I had to try out, of course.

"To Baja California, James, and don't spare the horses," I told her.

"Very good, sir. Will that be all, sir?"

"Yes, Jeeves. You can hang up, now. I'll call you back when we get to Los Angeles."

The car had such a long wheel base that Jean wouldn't ride in the back seat, because she got seasick when it went around corners. And John said he wouldn't drive the big hulk because he'd come along on the trip for a restful vacation, so Ed and I had agreed to spell each other at the wheel. We stacked the blanket rolls on the floor of the back compartment, over the two recessed jump seats that could pop up for extra passengers. John put his blanket roll on top of the pile, patted it, and Toby jumped up, stretched out, and, like a good dog, slept most of the way to Mexico and back. We found we had to talk mostly by telephone between the front and back sections. When the window was lowered it created such a draft and such an engine roar, that it was impossible to carry on conversations. We were in two separate island communities, which made it possible for only one-on-one conversations. Generally on this trip, Ed and I traded

HAND WRAP GIRL

places at the wheel from front to back, but occasionally, on straight highway runs, Jean would ride in back with John, and I'd get a chance to talk to Ed.

As we got under way down the Row, the sun was just lighting up the sky behind the dark silhouettes of the canneries. As we rolled along, somewhere in the midst of one of the dark buildings I remember seeing the searing blue star flash of an arc welder. Some poor guy was working late on a night shift, preparing the plant for the coming sardine packing season, still four months away.

We passed the Coast Guard Station and the stand of big cylindrical oil tanks on the shore. Some ten years earlier, in Monterey's biggest fire, a bolt of lightning had set them aflame and the oil had poured into the harbor, burning on the water amongst the boats. For safety's sake the majority of the tanks had been rebuilt in the sand dunes of Seaside, off on the horizon, on the other side of the bay.

In the morning light some of the boats were chugging out of the harbor with sports and market fishermen, but the majority of the larger purse seiners were away in

Alaska, fishing for salmon, or off to Oregon. At the wharf, a few tardy Sicillians in their bib overalls and floppy hip boots hurried along, their navy watch caps pulled down over their ears. Over their shoulders they carried the oars they needed to row their skiffs out to the larger boats, moored out by the breakwater. As we passed the ancient adobe Custom House, just beyond the wharf, we noticed it was too early for the dozen old retired fishermen, who usually sat there on the benches, waving their arms and arguing at the top of their voices. They always looked to me like they were playing a game of handball with an invisible ball.

In those days, before Highway One was carved through the impassable Big Sur area, in order to go south from Monterey, it was necessary to drive northeast to Salinas first, on the old back road. Then, north of Salinas, we turned south on 101—El Camino Real—the old Spanish King's Highway. First spaced out in the 1700s by the Franciscan padres, the missions were laid out in thirty mile intervals from San Diego north to Sonoma, like beads on a six hundred mile long rosary.

On the back road to Salinas John and I settled down to some serious conversation. I told John that as a kid I'd always wanted to be either an artist or a writer, and that I'd been slated to go to Stanford from a very young age, as was Jean. But then the Depression came along, and we both ended up at Berkeley, where the tuition was only twenty-five bucks a semester.

"Yeah, that's right," John admitted. "Tuition was always a tough nut to crack at a rich-kid's college like Stanford. I worked summers on ranches and my dad helped, but finances were a factor in my not graduating. Couple of times I dropped out for a whole semester and worked. I soon got to feeling Stanford wasn't teaching me anything about writing I couldn't learn myself."

John pointed out the window. "See that factory in the fields over there? That's the Spreckels Sugar Beet Factory. That's where I worked when I dropped out of Stanford, trying to make enough to take another run at it. I was an assistant chemist on the night shift. It was a darn good job because it gave me a chance to write during the daytime. I really enjoyed that job."

We stopped in Salinas at the old Hotel Cominos Coffee Shop just as it was opening, and had flapjacks and coffee. Then we drove on north toward the old brewery with its square tower on North Main. As we passed an old fashioned corner saloon, John pointed it out.

"There's the old bar I used for the setting of *Johnny Bear*."

I'd read the story in manuscript and liked it immensely. "I think that's one of your finest short stories, John. Did you ever know anybody who was a human sound recorder, like Johnny Bear?"

"No, I never did. Actually, I got the idea from an item in Ripley's *Believe it or Not!* And look, over there," John pointed to a large, gray Victorian house surrounded by a

"The Scientistos"
San Antonio Del Mar

cypress hedge, "That's the place I described as belonging to the two little old maids with the Chinese cook."

Just beyond that we turned right on to 101 and headed south. The road was much wider and Ed speeded up the big car. John and I settled back and began recalling, and laughing about a Lab beach picnic we'd been on a few months earlier. There must have been ten of us in the old Packard. It had all been very impromptu, on one of the few warm moonlight nights to hit the Monterey Peninsula. It was a lovely evening and the ocean looked so smooth that the better swimmers in the crowd began stripping to the buff for a moonlight skinny dip. Suddenly a big police car moved down the narrow night road toward us. Everybody had ducked out of the water and put on their clothes when they heard the sirens except for Jean. John muttered to me, "I'll get my sheepskin coat and see if I can head her off. Keep those cops interested with some story or other, and I'll see what I can do." When John came back, his trousers were wet to the waist where he'd walked out in the surf to give Jean his coat.

John asked me if I'd known a poet at Berkeley when I was on the staff of *The Occident*, a student named Howie Edminster.

"Sure did," I said. "He was damn good, too. One poem in particular was called "Each is Alone.""

"Yeah. That's the guy. He liked my stuff in the *Stanford Lit* and I liked his. We got together and enjoyed each other's company. He didn't look like any poet I'd ever met. Big, ugly cuss. Looked like a gangster. We both admired Hemingway's short story, *The Killers*. We'd pull our hats down over our eyes and slouch around The City thinking we looked like 'em. I sure got a kick out of old Howie. He was really outspoken and had a voice like a bullfrog. One time I took him over to meet a fancy-pants poet I'd met at an opening. This guy was a real la-de-da, if you know what I mean. He'd just come in from playing tennis with a couple of his rich old girl friends and he kept apologizing for not having had time to take a shower. 'But then again,' he says, 'Sometimes I like to perspire, don't

Ensenada - Naively Pretentious - 1936

Mexican government Mail Truck at San Antonio del Mar: One week from Tia Juana to San Lose del Cabo. May, 1936

you, Mr. Edminster?' 'Goddamn right,' Howie roars back. 'I like to STINK!' and he gets up and walks out on him."

John laughed so hard over his own story that his dog woke up and stared at him in concern. John patted his head until he went back to sleep again.

"What ever happened to your editor's job at *The Beacon?*" he asked me.

"It died and so did the magazine. Jean and I never got paid for all the work we did on it."

"Too bad. At least I got paid in horseback rides for my snake story."

"Yeah, but those horses didn't belong to the publisher. He was only boarding them for some Presidio cavalry officers who were away in Texas. They probably would have shot you for a horsethief if they'd come back and caught you on them."

"I'll be damned," John said, "I never knew that."

As we neared the little town of Greenfield, north of King City, John and I stopped our reminiscing because we both thought we smelled gasoline fumes. I picked up the intercom phone and buzzed Jean "on the bridge."

"Better tell Ed to stop up the road a bit. Smells funny back here. Leaking gasoline. We better check the load in back."

John took over the phone. "Yeah. Tell Ed there's a concrete overpass bridge up ahead. Stop just this side of it on the right. I'd like to show you something there."

Ed pulled the big car off the highway at the place John indicated and we got out to stretch our legs. Ed and I checked the gasoline tins. They seemed okay, although the ropes had loosened a bit. We snugged them up while John pointed below and told us, "Down there, by the river, is where I laid the scene for this book I'm proofing. It's the actual place, several years ago, where a posse caught up with this guy who murdered a farm girl, and shot him dead. I was working over that way, on a ranch, when it happened. That's what I plan to call this book: *Something That Happened*, or maybe, *A Thing That Happened*."

John and Jean went down the bank to look at the site where the man had been shot, while Ed and I fussed with the load on the back of the car. They came back in a few minutes and we drove on south toward King City.

"I think this will be an unusual book," John told me as we settled back. "Actually it's more of a play than a novel. I've always wanted to write a play, but since I'm a novelist, I thought doing a play in the form of a novel would be easier for me. And easier to reach my audience, and all without their going to the theatre. All the stage directions, the atmosphere, the implications are included as part of the story line in the novel. Does that make sense?"

"Sure. Shaw did the same sort of thing. Only he put all his philosophizing and all his social criticisms into long prefaces, which kept him from getting too preachy on stage."

"Right. But I'm thinking more along the lines of O'Neill's sea plays and *The Hairy Ape*. What O'Neill did for the American merchant sailor, I want to do for the American agriculture worker—the foot loose bindlestiff—who works from one ranch to another in harvest time. They are all dreaming of getting a little place of their own, like grown up orphans still looking for their father and mother's old home place."

He talked a little about his own Irish mother and his German father, both of whom had died only in the last year or so. The family name had originally been Grosssteinbeck, but they knocked of the first part when they came to America. His mother's family were the Hamiltons, from Northern Ireland.

"My mother's family were the Moriartys from the Southwest. If you and I were still in Ireland we'd probably be mortal enemies."

"Everyone in the Old World seems to be born hating each other," John said. "The Irish and the English. The Greeks and the Turks. The Arabs and the Jews. Now it's the Germans and the Italians in Spain, stirring up trouble between the Church and the Republicans. There's another World War coming. Believe it. Mussolini and Hitler are obviously testing their war machines. Sooner or later, we'll all be in it."

"God, I hope not," I said glumly. I stared out of the windows at the peaceful California hills carpeted in blue and gold wildflowers. South of King City we were skirting along William Randolph Hearst's enormous holdings. John said Hearst owned over a quarter of a million acres out there, clear to the Pacific. John had worked as a newspaper reporter for a short time in New York, on Hearst's *Journal American,* and he felt about him the way most young liberals of that era did. We all disliked Hearst, his lurid brand of journalism, and everything he stood for.

John told a funny story about the outraged old lady schoolteacher who comes to visit the father of one of her pupils. "Your son, little Billy, tells me that for a living, you play the piano in a whorehouse. I see that you're a very proper looking gentleman. Now, why would he want to say such a terrible thing like that about you?" The father looks embarrassed and says, 'Actually I work for the Hearst newspapers, but I couldn't tell my little boy that, now could I?' "

We had a good laugh, then John launched into the famous old story about Dorothy Parker trying to interview Hearst and his movie actress mistress, Marion Davies. I'd heard it before, and it was probably apocryphal, but I didn't stop him. John really enjoyed

telling his stories so much, and besides, I wanted to hear his version of it.

"So Dorothy Parker is supposed to do this *New Yorker* story on them," John went on. "But Hearst keeps her cooling her heels in this enormous antechamber full of religious statues. She sits there, smoking cigarettes and getting madder and madder. Finally she realizes she's just being put off, so she decides to leave, but before she does, she goes over to the big fancy guest book and writes this poem in it:

Upon my honor I saw a maddoner
Seated in a niche
Above the door of a prominent whore
And a well known
Sonofabitch!

John laughed so hard at his own story I thought he was going to choke to death. His dog awoke again and looked very concerned about him. John wiped the tears out of his eyes, comforted his dog with reassuring pats, and lit up a cigarette. John was a very heavy smoker (which very likely contributed to his relatively early death) and between puffs and gasps he went on to tell more stories about Hearst. John said the "old man" was like a big gray spider in the middle of his international news web. None of the reporters knew when he'd pounce on them. They were all running scared. Old Willy read everything they wrote and if he didn't like it, poof! Off with their heads! They were fired the next day. John said he finally got the bounce himself, because he wrote news stories like fiction, when the "old man" obviously wanted fiction written like news stories.

I told John about the time I did construction work for Hearst when I was about sixteen.

"I went to work for my dad on a demolition contract he had to knock down a big Irish castle on Hearst's Wyntoon Ranch. This castle was shaped just like a big black boot It had caught fire because all the seven floors were made of wood and they came crashing down inside. Hearst summoned his lady architect, Julia Morgan, and told her to design him another castle."

"I've heard about her," John said. "She's got a big summer place in Monterey. Over on the other side of the Presidio, on the polite site of Tortilla Flat. She designed all those big woodsy buildings at Asilomar."

"She's quite a character," I told him. "I suppose she's the first major architect in history who's also a woman. I got a chance to meet her at Wyntoon. She wore mannish clothes, smoked a cigar, and swore like a trooper. The four of us construction men were all husky outdoor types, and I figured she was showing off, throwing her weight around, trying to be one of the boys. I'd heard bad language all my

Mr John Steinbeck
Mexico - 1936
—bruce ariss

life on construction crews, but never from a woman before.

"Did you get to see old man Hearst?" John asked.

"Sure did. He was driven up in a big open touring car. He was sitting in the back seat with his arms over the shoulders of two movie stars, one on each side of him. One I recognized as Marion Davies. He stared at us for a long time while we walked on the old wood-burning steam shovel that was knocking down the castle. An old fireman standing next to me on the rig said he hated the sight of Hearst because he'd been badly burned in an industrial accident working on Hearst's old *Call-Bulletin* steam presses before the war. He claimed the paper never paid him any compensation or helped on the doctor bills. I practically had to restrain the old guy from picking up a log to heave at the publisher."

John said that a bureaucrat friend of his in Sacramento had told him that Hearst had taken out licenses for twenty-one machine guns that he'd set up around his San Simeon castle. John said the old guy was obviously expected the Red Revolution to happen any day now, but he shouldn't believe everything he read in the Hearst newspapers.

South of King City, skirting Hearst's country, the scenery was all green rolling hills covered with spring sunshine and purple and gold wildflowers. The pale yellow wild mustard blossoms streamed away to the horizon southward, as though made by a giant brushstroke. I remembered reading somewhere that Father Serra and his Franciscans had scattered mustard seeds as they traveled north, so they'd be able to return the same way they came, along a yellow blazed pathway, the following spring.

John and I had talked ourselves out for the moment. We dozed for a bit while the big Packard droned southward. It occurred to me sleepily that I had planned to get John to do most of the talking, but he constantly seemed to be pumping me instead.

Southward, beyond Hearst country, the low hills seemed endless. In the front seat of the Packard, ahead of the chauffeur's glass wall, we could hear the murmur of the motor, and Jean and Ed chatting away quietly. We couldn't hear what they were saying, but from the cadence of their voices, I presumed they were quoting or talking poetry.

Jean had recently introduced Ed into the world of poetry she loved so much. He was a scientist, and I suppose it was a field he hadn't been particularly interested in before. Jean had memorized a great deal of Robinson Jeffers' work and Ed was so impressed by it he went out and bought all of Jeffers' books he could find. Ed seemed intrigued by the poet's concept of "breaking through" or, as Jeffers phrased it, "slitting the blind mask" that prevents us from seeing the world inside us, as well as around us.

John, myself, and the dog, lulled by the motor and the murmur of their voices, drowsed away in the back seat until we finally reached civilization. Ed pulled into the red, white, and blue Standard Oil Company gas station at the pier in Santa Barbara about mid-afternoon. While the car was being serviced, Jean, John, and Ed got out to

Ensenada

"El jusgado" Ensenada 1936

stretch their legs. I made my first sketch of the three of them from the back seat.

Ed swung the car down a side street of Santa Barbara and stopped in front of an ancient one story adobe building that obviously dated back to the Mexican California era.

"We better get used to home made Mexican food," Ed said. "This place has marvelous cheese enchiladas."

It was a simple little family restaurant, clean and cool, run by a fat cheerful Mexican mother and her slender teen-aged daughter. Ed was certainly right about the enchiladas. They were delicious. We ate all we could hold, washing them down with ice cold Mexican beer. Jean ordered Coca Cola. She hadn't learned to drink alcoholic beverages yet. She was still intimidated by her father's thundering farewell edict: "The first sip of beer you take is the first step down the primrose path to hell!"

After lunch I offered to drive south to Los Angeles, but Ed said he was okay and knew all the shortcuts through the traffic. John fed Toby some dog food, and some of the Mexican table scraps he saved, and we started off again.

John and I talked a bit about our fathers, and how they reacted to our choice of professions. Because I was obsessed with drawing from the time I was a little kid, my tough old Scotch father decided arbitrarily that I was to become an architect. I tried architecture for six months before switching to fine arts because I felt that architecture was superfluous in the Depression 30s. Almost half the buildings in Berkeley were for rent. The students were living in empty storefronts and had built their own Pipe City in the big concrete water pipe sections waiting to be installed underground in Berkeley. Who needed an architect?

John said his father had wanted him to become a lawyer, but he was only interested in writing, and his father had finally come to accept it pretty well.

Just north of Los Angeles, about sunset, Ed had steered into an unfamiliar and rather singular suburb. He seemed to know where he was going. It was in the days before the freeways, when everyone had his own secret route through the back streets of the big city maze. I've never been able to find this strange suburb since.

Everything about it seemed to be made of a garish pink stucco. So garish, in fact, that the inhabitants must have suffered attacks of nausea and fled the place. All the large, pink-walled pink-tiled houses had faded "For Sale" signs on them. Even the sidewalks and curbs were pink cement. Only the asphalt streets were black, probably because they'd yet to find a way to dye asphalt paving pink.

The poles of the street lights were also pink and, as we drove through, the lights came on suddenly against the pink of the sunset sky. No lights in the silent mansions came on. We conjectured this was some sort of wealthy confectioner's pink frosted housing project that had been finished just before the Crash, some six years earlier, and

Drawn by little boy bootblack in Tia Juana 1936

none of the expensive looking homes had ever sold in the shrivelling Depression economy.

John rapped on the chauffeur's window and pointed to his dog. Ed nodded and pulled over to a pink curb and stopped the car. We all got out to stretch our legs while the dog stained the pink lamp post pinker. Even the air seemed thick and pink from the sunset glow. Ed turned off the engine and there wasn't a sound.

"Isn't this weird?" Ed said. "It's like it's the end of the world."

"Gabriel's horn should sound any second now," Jean agreed. "Wouldn't this make a great sunset backdrop for the Second Coming?"

"Enter the Messiah, stage left," I said.

"Talk about your Pipe City!" John chuckled. "This is Pipe Dream City. A pink ghost town! What's the name of this place?"

"San or Santa something or other," Ed said. "There was a sign on an abandoned real estate office back there."

"How about Santa Cerise?" I suggested.

"Or San Fiasco," John added.

We climbed back into the car and Ed threaded his way down through the darkening streets of Los Angeles. He parked on Olvera Street, in the Mexican section, and we dined on tacos in an open air makeshift street booth. By the light of hanging Coleman lanterns I made another quick sketch. Then Ed drove us on to the seashore at Corona Del Mar. He pulled into the beachfront parking area behind the darkened Scripps Institute Oceanography buildings.

We went inside a big warehouse filled with concrete holding tanks, like the ones Ed had built behind his own Lab. The people on the night shift all knew Ed, were glad to see him, and showed us around. I made some quick sketches of the marine life in the tanks, the same sort of specimens Ed said we planned to collect in Mexico.

A young graduate student shoved the handle of a broom into one of the open tanks.

"Here's what you should watch out for when you're collecting in Mexican waters," he said. A huge, gray greenish Moray eel, four feet long, lunged out of the dark water and clamped its crooked teeth around the stick. Its close set eyes gleamed malevolently as it worried the broom stick back and forth in bulldog fashion.

"Wow!" I said. "What would that bastard have done to my fingers?"

"What fingers?" the graduate student replied.

It was a balmy night on the beach. We lit our two Coleman lanterns, but decided against starting a fire. It was too warm and we were too tired. We laid out our blanket rolls with our heads against an overturned lifeboat. John tossed and turned for a few minutes on the hard packed sand, then picked up his bedroll and said he was going to sleep in the back seat of the Packard.

"I better keep my pup company," he decided. "He might run off in the night."

For myself, I was so tired I was sure I could have slept on an iron plate. I guess we all dropped off to sleep very quickly. I was awakened by the bright light of the dawn and rolled over on my elbow to inspect the beach. Another over-sized example of Southern California architecture blocked out the sunrise that was brightening the sky. There was a small hill beyond the cove, across from where we were camping, that loomed over this strange structure.

It was four-story concrete Chinese pagoda, over-sized and ridiculous looking. It was painted orange and had a green-tiled roof with exaggerated turned up corners. On the small sandy hill above it, was perched a silly-looking oriental gazebo, or outhouse, which seemed to be staring blindly out to sea toward China. Probably, I thought, searching in vain for its distant Eastern derivatives.

I grinned and made a quick sketch of this bit of orange stucco splendor. While I was drawing, the Anglo-looking householder, in pale green pajamas, emerged from a second floor doorway and struggled down a long ramp with an overloaded garbage can. He set it down noisily by the basement garage doors. Then he opened the big doors, went inside, and started his car. After a few minutes of warming the engine, he drove a large black Rolls Royce limousine out onto the apron in front of the garage. He shut off the motor, got out, and began to lovingly polish the big car in the sunrise light. No doubt, I thought with amusement, these must be the strange early-morning religious rituals of the local Green-Pajama natives.

Steinbeck was still asleep in the Packard, his big feet sticking out of the open rear window. I dressed, went over, and sat down to make a sketch of him against the

Typical Baja Scene 1936

background of the Institute building. Beyond was the breakwater and a busy traffic of fishing boats moving out of the harbor.

John awoke, saw me sketching him, and grinned. He put on his socks and boots and came over, buttoning up his shirt and pants, to check on my drawing.

"Those are my feet, all right," he admitted. Toby, freed from the car, took off down the beach after a local shepherd pup. The two of them bounced along in the surf, obviously delighted in their frolic.

"Guess I'll start a fire and make the coffee," John said, walking off toward the lifeboat. Jean was still asleep in its shadow and Ed had disappeared, probably visiting the morning crew in the Scripps warehouse. Toby came back out of the water, looking like a large, skinny, wet rat. He shook himself, sprinkling Jean, who woke up protesting.

"That damn dog! I like a cold shower in the morning, but not a second-hand one!"

She dressed and started the bacon and eggs over the little fire John had built of driftwood. Ed came back just as we were sitting down to eat. Over the leisurely breakfast we discussed the plans for the day.

"We're only going a few miles south of here," Ed told us. "To La Jolla beach. A good collecting spot."

We loaded up our camping gear, and this time I drove the car, with Jean in front and John and Ed in back with the dog.

When we were cruising down the highway Jean said, "John certainly seems to be in an exceptionally good mood on this trip, doesn't he? What did you two talk about all day yesterday?"

"Mostly about the crazy architecture we passed. Then we exchanged tall stories. You know, trying to outdo each other, topping each other's crazy stories about old Willy Hearst. What did you and Ed talk about?"

"About his three kids. And poetry. And his scientific theories. He never stops talking about them, you know."

"I know. But it's sure a lot better than staying home and listening to the radio spout all the bad news about the wars in Spain or Manchuria or Africa. John and Ed both think another World War's inevitable."

"God, I hope not," Jean sighed. "It's all so ridiculous. Stupid. Grown men playing at little boys' shoot-em-up games. As if we don't have enough trouble trying to stay alive in this miserable Depression."

"The thing is, when there's a war, everyone goes to work making arms to kill each other off, and suddenly there's no more Depression. Isn't there an old Chinese saying about burning down the barn in order to get a good dinner of roast pig?"

"Are you sure that wouldn't be lamb?" Jean asked.

We set up camp late that afternoon on the rocky La Jolla beach. It was to be our first night of collecting marine specimens on the trip. We made coffee and washed down thick white bread and baloney sandwiches. Then we checked our gear. Hip boots, buckets, jute sacks, jars, trays, and so on. After sundown, Ed lit the two Coleman lanterns. The tide had receded far out into the night horizon, exposing the dark and glistening tide pools.

The four of us began our collecting. As I remember, we were selecting mostly brittle-stars, a slender-armed little starfish-like creature. I saw something larger moving in the shadow of a rock. Forgetting the Scripps student's warning, I grabbed for it. Fortunately it was not a Moray eel, but a small octopus, about twenty-four inches in diameter. It wrapped its tentacles around my wrist and arm, struggling to break from my grasp.

"Hey, Ed!" I yelled in some alarm. "I've caught an octopus! Will it bite?"

"No, no. Hang on to it!" Ed hurried up with a jute sack. He disengaged the writhing creature and shoved it deftly into the sack. "Good work! A fine specimen! No, octopi won't attack warm-blooded animals. (Ed pronounced it OK-TOE-PEE.) It was probably a lot more frightened of you

Mexican Master Carpenter & Assistant

Jean's New Sombrero — Tia Juana

than you were of him. They're very shy and very intelligent, and difficult to capture. Excellent! This will be the best catch of the evening, I'm sure."

It was the one and only octopus we encountered on the entire trip, though John was to write later that we spent a week collecting octopi in Baja.

We worked on through the night until the tide started to return. Then Ed called it off, emptying the buckets of specimens into large flat trays of seawater. The four of us found we were exhausted from the hours of concentrated stoop labor amongst the slippery rocks. We unrolled our blankets on a sandy stretch above the high-tide line.

Ed turned off the glaring lanterns and it was surprising how black the night was. In a little while our eyes adjusted to the starlight. The sound of the pounding surf roiling the grapefruit-sized rocks together on the beach was more difficult to accept, but after a few moments even this giant grinding of the ocean's teeth faded away into our deep sleep.

The following morning we awoke with the sunrise, made a quick campfire breakfast, then loaded up our gear and headed southward. Ed drove on through San Diego without stopping. I remember passing a big old house with a sign on it saying this was the place where Helen Hunt Jackson had written *Ramona*. There was some sort of annual fiesta going on, with a parade, but Ed managed to skirt the crowds and we weren't held up by it. We reached the Mexican border and passed through the inspection station with no problems. The officials knew Ed from previous trips and waved us on through into Tiajuana.

Tiajuana, in 1936, was a sleazy little town of shacks and unpainted shops. It's sole reason for existence seemed to be to unload junky souvenirs on Yankee tourists. Everything about the town seemed to be in falling-down disrepair. Every ancient automobile, too decrepit to sell in the States, had apparently managed a sort of reverse-wetback trip across the border in search of impoverished owners in Mexico. We parked and walked along the tacky little main street, inspecting the shops.

Ed decided Jean should have one of the big Mexican

straw hats with the wide brims to protect her from the sun. John and I finally tired of her seemingly endless trying on of hats. We decided we'd stroll around town, then meet them back at the car. Shortly after we emerged from the shop into the sharp sunlight, an engaging, bright-eyed little Mexican kid accosted us. He was a bootback, barefooted himself, but with a big wooden box of shoe brushes and polishes hanging over his shoulder by a strap. He was probably seven or eight years old. He jabbered away at us in a wild mix of Spanish and English.

"Allo, aye paqueets! Jouwanna shoes eschined?"

"Your Spanish is better than mine," I said to John. "What the hell's he saying?"

"That's supposed to be English," John decided. "I think he said, 'Hello, High Pockets. Do you want your shoes shined?'"

"Oh! No, sorry, kid. You can't shine these old work boots of mine. They're too beat up. Too rough. Same with his. You savvy?"

"Sure. That's okay. Hey, mister, you draw pitch?"

The boy reached up brashly and took the big sketch book from under my arm. He inspected the sketches, nodding his head in approval. Then he grinned up at me and held out his hand.

"You gimme pencil. I draw pitch, too."

Amused, I handed him one of the big Eagle draughting pencils I always carried in my shirt pocket. He turned to an unused page in the back of the book. With amazing deftness he sketched the profile of a man's head.

"Hey, that's very good," I told him. *Muy bueno. Damn fine pitch."

John agreed and flipped him a dime, the equivalent of two shoe shines. The boy ran off happily.

"That kid's all right," John said. "He's got the makings of a real artist. Most little *Norte Americano* kids his age would draw Mickey Mouse or Popeye. He's drawn a perfect Mexican Indian profile, like those old Mayan heads. Pretty damned good!" John said he felt like chasing the kid down and trying to get him a scholarship to the great Mexican State Peasants' University—"Peon U."

We found Ed and Jean back at the car, waiting for us. Ed said he was anxious to get underway for our next collecting beach. He told us it was just outside of Ensenada, the nearest town beyond Tiajuana to the south. All Saints Beach, I think he called it. *Todos Santos.* He felt we ought to get there as soon as possible, to set up camp before the sun went down.

We climbed back into the Packard and drove off southward on the first, last, and only piece of good roadway we were to find in Baja. It was a strip of brand new blacktop, narrow, without a painted center line, and as smooth as glass. It looked like it had just been finished that very morning and ours was the first car to use it.

The new road was so smooth and T-square straight that Jean decided there wouldn't be any danger of her getting carsick if she rode in back with John for a change. Ed stopped the big old Packard, right in the center of that long perspective of black asphalt, and we got out and traded places.

I hadn't had much chance to talk to Ed so far, on this trip. Besides, this would give me the opportunity to do a sketch of him as we toured smoothly along. Ed had a very sensitive profile. Delicate, but not effeminate. I couldn't quite catch it.

He surprised me by suddenly saying, "You know, of course, that I'm falling in love with that Jean of yours? She's such an incredibly pure and wonderful girl I can't believe she's real."

"I know what you mean," I said, rather uncomfortably. That lunatic Ed was always so damned straightforward about coming out with things that other people would have left unsaid. I thought his remark disarmingly honest, but painfully revealing. Jean always said that the only difference between John and Ed was Ed couldn't tell a lie and John couldn't tell the truth. Ed's remark was somewhat embarrassing to me as her husband, and for a moment I was at a loss as to how to answer his question. If it was a question.

"Well, Ed, you're not the only one. You'll just have to stand in line. During one of our first outings together, I heard a loud voice inside my head telling me that I was going to spend the rest of my life with her. It was wierd. Like a huge voice over a loudspeaker. Do you believe that?"

"I certainly do. The brain has billions of individual cells, like amoebae. Brain cells have specialized for hundreds of millions of years, just to follow electrical and chemical impulses that are atom-small and come from everywhere. One normal human brain has far more hookups and connections than all the switchboards in the world rolled into one. Science has only just begun to study such complexity and already they're saying *anything is possible*."

"What ever happened in those experiments you were doing with amoeba?"

"Oh, yes! The amoebae. Magnificent little organisms!" Ed was off and running on one of his favorite themes. He loved to talk about nature. He was a born teacher. Ed should have been a professor. "Have you ever seen an amoeba under a really fine microscope?"

"No."

"It looks exactly like a transparent and mobile little sack of jewels. Marvelously multi-colored jewels that are always moving in slow motion. Moving this way and that, for no apparent reason. Then suddenly one of the little jewels seems to take a direction. It moves toward the wall of the sac. Or is it, perhaps, pushed in that direction by other molecules? In any case, it's tiny pressure on the wall causes an outward bulge and a pseudopodia is formed. A false foot. The foot becomes larger. The nearby particles seem to become excited and they move off in that direction, too. In that fashion, the amoeba constantly travels through its environment, here and there, searching for its sustenance, which it neatly encircles and absorbs."

"Sounds fascinating."

"It is. But the question that actually fascinates me is, what determines its direction? As I said, one of the little molecular jewels puts pressure on the wall to form the foot. Can we consider this molecule the leader of the others? Or does it just happen accidentally to be in the way? In the forefront? Or is it simply moved by the pressure from behind it?"

"You're drawing a parallel to human leadership, of course?" I said. "And large population movements, too? The Forty-Niners crossing the plains in their wagons?"

"Of course! The future of each one of these little single-celled universes depends on its direction. It may be propelled into an area where there's insufficient nutrients, or it's too hot or too cold. For example, if you take a circular culture dish containing amoebae, warm it gently in a band across the center, and cool it at the top and bottom edges, the amoebae will line up in two strips across the dish. They're seeking what is called their optimum—the best possible environment for their particular form of life."

"I see. Very much like the human population in the various zones of the earth."

"Exactly. In the temperate zones we have the world's two largest bands of population. At the equator, or in the arctic and antarctic, the population thins out."

"What you're saying is that all those amoebas in that dish, like the humans on this earth, are instinctively seeking their optimum—in the temperate zones, where there's plenty of food and nutrients?"

"That's it precisely. You've grasped the implication very quickly. As a younger man, I came to this same conclusion. Not without some difficulty, and over a period of years. My most inspiring teacher was a man named Alee, at the University of Chicago. I was also deeply influenced by the writings of John Boodin on cosmic evolution. The microcosm duplicates the macrocosm. Each microscopic single-celled animal is like a galaxy of stars—or, by further extension, all the galaxies that make up the universe."

"Or all the universes," I said, taking it one step farther. "That could make up some sort of ultra-universe."

"Excellent thought," Ed conceded, nodding his head.

One of Ed's most extraordinary attributes, according to all his friends, was that he made them feel *intelligent*. It was a Socratic device of his, I suppose, but you always came away from a conversation with him thinking you were not so stupid after all. Ed admired the way you thought. He accepted your contributions seriously. He turned your ideas this way and that, enhancing them, making them seem a lot more important than you expected them to be.

I don't think he did this consciously, or to be manipulative. He was just so excited by abstract ideas that his mind instantly took off with yours, exploring in every direction. There was one problem that was bothering me, however. One that I hadn't had the chance to open up with him before. I plunged into it.

"At Cal I had a teacher named Frederick Teggart. His ideas seem to me to be in almost direct opposition to your Alee's. He hated what he called the Biological Analogy."

"Why is that?"

"Well, Teggart says that the Biological Analogy is one of the great fallacies in the thinking of modern man, because humans, though they are animals, don't behave like animals. They've developed into a new form of life. One that has an intellect which allows it to visualize and plan its own direction. To intentionally change its own environment—its own way of life."

"That's true, of course," Ed conceded. "But man's intellect is such a Johnny-come-lately in the evolutionary scheme of things. How important is it, really? Does he direct his life, or is it vice-versa? What was it Thoreau said about most men leading lives of quiet desperation? Isn't it because they're operating on a behavior pattern that's fundamentally instinctive, and beyond their control? All life operates on energy. Unthinking, random energy that has derived fundamentally from the forces of the sea. Wave motion gave life its original direction. It's built into every one of our cells. Blood and sea water have the same specific gravity. In a sense, we are giant, mobile sacs of sea water, still nourishing all our trillions of cells from the inside of the sac. That's a pretty basic inheritance. Life in tide pools reproduces at low tide,

ORIENTAL SPLENDOR CORONA DEL MAR 1936

which, of course, is dependent on the twenty-eight day cycle of the moon. For example, as the tide goes out, the pressure is lowered and the eggs burst from the turgid starfish. Human females, in their monthly menstrual cycles, also operate on a lunar time table. I'm sure you know how unreasonable a woman can get in her menstrual period. She's certainly not operating on intellect then, but on an ancient and inherited chemical reaction straight out of the tidal seas of the beginning of time."

"A very interesting sequence of ideas," I admitted. "But they're all based on your scientific experience. Professor Teggart, as a historian, has come up with quite a different set of concepts."

"For example?"

"He said that Western man is basically schizoid, because his ideas come from two very different cultures—the Greeks and the Jews. The Greeks were agrarians, and each year they planted the seeds of their corn, watched the plants slowly mature, then dry up and die. The following year they planted more seeds and the process was repeated exactly. The Greeks had many gods, but as an agricultural people they were most interested in the worship of Demeter, the goddess of the corn. By corn, they meant wheat, of course. Our corn comes from the New World Indians."

"Go on."

"The Greeks' scientific thinking revolved around the growth cycle and the inevitability of the return of the seasons. They even believed there was a great cycle of history, which was repeated again and again, just as the corn plant repeats itself. So Socrates would drink another bowl of hemlock, in some future but identical market place, many times over. Teggart says that the Greek way of thinking has given rise to modern scientific thought, which is based essentially on the cycle."

"Very interesting," Ed nodded thoughtfully again. "And what did he say about the Jews?"

"The Jews, on the other hand, led an entirely different life. They were nomadic herdsmen. There was nothing cyclical about their lives. The wolves quite unexpectedly came down on the fold and killed their sheep. Sudden storms blew away their tents. They died of unexplained illnesses. Their land was a military crossroads between the east and the west. The armies of the Persians, or the Greeks, marched through ancient Israel alternately, but erratically, laying waste to everything with their scorched earth policies. The Jews' God was Jehovah, a miserable tyrant, a surly father figure, full of jealous wrath, who struck them down for fancied insults, or for minor sins, or for no reason at all. All they could do about it was chronicle what happened, and who begat whom. They became historians—the first historians of the Western World, just as the Greeks were the first scientists. These two opposing kinds of thinking, the cyclical and the episodic, are what's confusing us so badly today."

"I see. And what are Teggart's conclusions?"

"Only that modern man has a bellyache, or a headache, rather, because he's been unable to absorb or digest these two conflicting systems of thinking. We can't seem to separate them, so we try to operate with both. It's like a bicycle with one round wheel and one square wheel. It just won't ride. President Hoover said not to worry about the Depression. It's cyclical. It'll be over soon. It'll take care of itself. Prosperity is just around the corner. But President Roosevelt says it's an unusual and singular misfortune that's struck us like a bolt of lightning from above. Probably caused by the collapse of international banking due to gambling on Wall Street for paper profits, and other such sins. We've got to do something about it. Anything. Declare a Bank Holiday. Inaugurate the NRA. Prime the economic pump with lots of government funds, doled out through the CCC, the WPA, and so on. Trouble is, most politicians try to sponsor both opposing philosophies. 'Let's fight this great Depression that's come out of nowhere. It's unprecedented, but if we use all the economic tools available, we can get back on the track, into our old, healthy cycle again.' "

"Hm, that's interesting." I could see Ed was trying honestly to think about a philosophy that was foreign to his own way of looking at the world. "Does Teggart have any books published?"

"He made a syllabus for his sociology course, but he kept referring to a monumental work on the philosophy of history that he's been working on for years. His plan is to pursue all the ideas of our modern world back through history to their origins in tribal times."

"That's a colossal project!" Ed whistled, and shook his head. "You said he was a very old man? He'll never make it!"

The discussion was cut short quite suddenly when we hit a huge chuckhole at the end of the smooth pavement. We had arrived at Ensenada already! That long, smooth, straight-arrow highway seemed to have cut the trip to almost nothing.

We inspected the town with some curiosity and agreed it was a far better place than Tiajuana. It was cleaner, more permanent looking, although it, too, plainly showed that the Depression must have hit hard on all these towns below the border. Most of the automobiles seemed to be dilapidated rejects from old Southern Californian used car lots. I sketched one ancient Model T coupe going by with a sad-faced burro tied in a home-made pickup box on the back. Obviously, John said, for an auxiliary engine in case of a breakdown.

Many of the adobe houses were disintegrating badly at this time in Baja. Since they were made of mud bricks, any leaking roofs that went unattended for very long resulted in water-soaked and collapsed walls. Many of the roofs on the outskirts of town were made of thatch. If the winds blew away the thatching, the mud structures rapidly returned to the surrounding earth from which they were formed.

There were adobes dotting the landscape in all stages of collapse, down to grassy humps that must have once been buildings. Right in Ensenada I saw one quite large adobe with its roof completely gone, and the walls worn away by erosion. And the building still seemed to be

Steinbeck Asleep — CORONA DEL MAR 8:00 am TUESDAY

ABALONE DIVER in Big Sur 1937

inhabited. Three women draped in heavy black shawls sat on the steps with their dog, and all four of them stared at me impassively as I made a quick sketch of them. None moved a muscle. It was though they were posing for an old-fashioned, time-exposure, tin-type photograph.

The only evidence of any actual construction I saw I recorded in an amusing little sketch. At the building site of a small new adobe house I started to draw the builder and his ten year old barefoot assistant, but as soon as I sat down to sketch them, they quit work and walked off. John said it was probably siesta time. The builder obviously considered himself a master carpenter. He was very jauntily dressed, wore a snap-brim hat, a mustachio with waxed ends, a white shirt and necktie, and a bulky brown leather apron that almost touched the ground. As he walked pompously away toward town, ignoring us, I noticed he carried his badge of office, a yellow wooden folding foot rule, like a baton, held out in front of him.

I told John an American carpenter would have been laughed off the job in a costume like that. His barefoot boy assistant, like a caddy, staggered way behind him, carrying all the loose tools from the job in his arms. He stared back after us, probably wondering what we were grinning about.

I next asked Ed to stop the car for a minute while I sketched a large garishly pink public building on the waterfront. It appeared to be in exceptionally good repair. It looked like the foreign legion fortress in the movie, *Beau Geste*. Rifle slots enfiladed the walls all around, like a lace decoration. John said it was *El Jusgado*, the jailhouse, and that this Spanish word was the source of the slang "hoosegow," the term used for a jail by cowboys throughout the American Southwest. A few seedy-looking policemen, in mustard-colored military uniforms, lounged against the pink walls, smoking and trying to keep in the shade.

We moved on into town where I drew what I thought was an amusing example of naively pretentious architecture. It was a two-story false front building with a precarious-looking balcony tacked across its front. It had a tin lookout cupola for a third floor. It was painted in marvelously faded bands of color: grayed white, pink, and red-brown. It would have made a fine water color, if only I'd brought my paint box along. I jotted down notes about the colors on the sketch, hoping to do a water color when I got back to Monterey, but fifty years have gone by and I've yet to do it.

I wrapped up my sketching with this one, as everyone seemed to be famished. All their discussion about food started my own stomach growling. We parked and went into a small, white-painted, wooden restaurant with large windows that looked out on to the ultramarine waters of the Pacific. Small white fishing boats dotted the deep blue expanse all the way to the horizon.

We ordered swordfish, since that was the major sportfish of the harbor. We were served steaming fist-sized portions of the flaky white meat, along with large boiled potatoes and stacks of warm and delicious tortillas. The fish was so savory I've been ordering swordfish in Stateside restaurants ever since, but none has ever tasted as good. It was so fresh it must have been dragged out of the water and into the kitchen of the cafe, just as we entered the front door.

The tortillas were particularly good, too. Ed asked if we could buy some to take along. The buxom young waitress shook her head, but managed to explain that they came from a bakery right next door. We drank the excellent black coffee, but didn't touch the fruit the girl brought for dessert. This tasty meal cost about two pesos each, and the exchange rate then was running about six Mexican pesos to one American dollar.

After this savory lunch we went next door to the bakery and watched an elderly woman slap-slapping tortillas from hand to hand. We bought a stack one foot high which she wrapped in newspaper. We next went to the *carneceria*, where Ed bought a yard long chain of *chorizos*, the Mexican spicy-hot chile sausages.

"It's the only meat down here you dare eat," Ed explained with a chuckle. "The chile is so fierce it sterilizes all the old contaminated meat they make them with. And it'll do the same to you if you take too big a bite of them."

We drove down to the abandoned lighthouse on the beach, with its truncated tower, and set up our camp in front of it. Ed said he'd heard the big French polished glass beacon that used to be on top of the building had been relocated farther down the coast, because there were more shipwrecks down there where there was no light. Ed thought that quite a choice bit of Mexican logic.

Jean said she was still exhausted from collecting the night before, and was going to try to catch a few winks before going to work again. I made two quick sketches of her as she gradually folded over for a catnap before sunset. We worked late again in the night tidepools, but for the life of me, I can't remember now what specimens we collected on that particular beach.

For sunrise breakfast we had tortillas and chile sausages. Ed was so right! The *chorizos* were unbelievably hot and spicy. The water we tried to quench them down with tasted strongly of gasoline and formaldehyde. "Not the tastiest goddamn breakfast in the world," I thought, but didn't say anything. No doubt the others were getting the same reaction from their assorted and assaulted stomachs.

"We'll stop at this little winery in Santo Tomas," Ed said. "They make a very cheap, very good claret. Then we won't have to drink this tinned water anymore."

"But I can't stand wine, either," Jean complained. "Do you think I can buy some Coca-Cola at the winery?"

"Well, I'm not sure," Ed smiled. "But I doubt it very much."

Beyond Ensenada the bad roads began. Or rather, the road seemed to disappear entirely. There was a broad, sandy plain south of the little town with hundreds of tire tracks criss-crossing it in all directions. I was driving and tried to choose the best-looking tracks heading south. I also had to keep the car moving fairly fast, for I was afraid if we slowed down we would get stuck in the sand. The long car pitched and rolled, exactly like a ship at sea.

Jean, at my side in the front passenger seat, suddenly began making frantic gestures. She clapped one hand over her mouth and pointed outside with the other, indicating I had to let her out so she could throw up. I managed to park on a grass-covered knoll so we'd have a chance to get a running start again. Jean dashed out and walked back and forth over the sand, fighting her sea-sickness. After a bit she said she felt better, but decided she would try riding outside in the open, lying on her stomach on top of one of the big front spare tires in the right fender well.

As the big car ate up the miles southward, the terrain gradually elevated into a low plateau that skirted the shoreline. The maze of tire tracks that had webbed the sandy plain settled into a single pair that seemed to know where it was going. Jean signaled she'd had enough of the outdoors. I stopped the car with the front wheels resting in a clear stream of water that trickled out of the brushy hinterlands on our left, across the road, and spilled over the bluff on the right side, into the ocean below.

"I feel much better now," Jean said. "But it's getting awfully warm, isn't it? Doesn't that water look delicious? I haven't had a decent drink of water since we left the States. That canned junk we brought along is terrible. Ed, I'm getting awfully thirsty. Don't you think I can drink out of this stream? It looks so pure."

"I wouldn't risk it, if I were you," Ed cautioned.

"But then, you're not me," Jean suddenly decided. She threw herself face down beside the stream and drank deeply. "It tastes absolutely marvelous! Try some, Bruce."

"No thanks," I said. "I admit it looks inviting, but I think I'll play it safe and stick to our artificially flavored stuff."

Feeling much refreshed, Jean said she was going to follow the stream inland to stretch her legs. John and I accompanied her while Ed dipped up some of the water for the car's radiator.

Thirty feet from where we stopped the car, around the first bend of the rivulet, we came on a gruesome sight. A dead black and white cow, bloated and covered with a cloud of blow flies, was lying half buried in the water. Poor Jean! She gasped, then dashed into the bushes and heaved. I'm sure the chile sausages were even worse coming back up than going down.

"Do you think she's poisoned? I asked Ed, who had joined us and was staring at the dead cow.

"Well, I don't think so," Ed said. "Running water cleanses itself of impurities very quickly. I'm sure it was just the sight of that miserable carrion that turned her stomach."

"From the sound of it," John said with some sympathy, "Any bugs she might have swallowed for the past year have all been retched out of her."

We drove on southward, following the two tire tracks through the brush, without ever meeting another car. The road now swerved inland, away from the coast, and climbed slowly into a low and barren mountain range. The dirt road was better engineered here, and though steep, gracefully snaked upward until we reached the summit of the Santo Tomas range. I stopped the car to give it a chance to cool off and we looked down into the valley at the small green patch of village below. I made a quick sketch of the view while we waited for the car to cool.

Ed took the wheel for the long drive down into Santo Tomas. I climbed in back with John again, and he told me that Ed and he had been having a stimulating discussion on the possibilities of racial memory. John had been skeptical and argued that Ed's ideas went counter to all recognized scientific evidence. The processes learned by one generation were not transmittable to the next one—at least not by any known changes in the inheritance. Man had managed to solve the problem by communication: speech, recorded science, history, and so on, but the lower animals couldn't.

What Ed was apparently talking about was an actual memory of the environment of previous generations. For example, Ed told him there was one famous case involving an American girl of Scottish descent, who became hysterical while visiting an old castle in Scotland. She insisted there was a door in a blank stone wall where none was visible. They finally broke down the wall and discovered a secret chamber with a skeleton chained in it. John wanted to know what I thought of Ed's yarn. Was it just another ghost story? Or was there really such a thing as racial memory?

I said it sounded more like a tourists' bureau

"Tendajon" Santo Tomas

concoction to me, but I had noticed that most of the ethnic immigrant groups that came to America seemed to settle in a climate identical to that of their homeland. The Mexicans and Spanish in the Southwest, the Swedes in Minnesota, the Irish in Boston and San Francisco, and so on. Maybe that could be a racial memory, too, left over from hundreds of generations spent in such familiar climates?

John wasn't sure that was what Ed meant. There was something more mystical and supernatural about it the way Ed had put it. Ed's thoughts were always elliptical and hard to grasp. A sort of scientific speculation that didn't seem to make much sense when he first broached his ideas to you. Ed had an offbeat earnestness about him that made you feel that was what he was telling you was damned important, and not at all as incredulous as it first sounded.

"He's like Einstein," John said. "You feel he's trying to tell you something remarkable, but it's up there in a cloud, over your head. Einstein's relativity theories sounded like black magic at first, too, but it's since turned out they're only corrections on old Newtonian physics. Pragmatic adjustments to take care of modern atomic speeds, and so on, right?"

"Yeah, I think that's it," I agreed. "But Ed's something more than that. I've heard he actually corresponds with Krishnamurti, the Hindu mystic. He borders on eastern mysticism, himself, you know. He's done a lot of reading in occult Indian philosophy all of which is so damn foreign to our Western mechanistic way of thinking."

"I know all that," John said.

"Yes, but here's an item I bet you don't know. Ed's practiced those Eastern arts himself. Jean told me she was asking him about levitation, and he actually demonstrated it. Assumed the lotus position and then lifted himself right up off the floor!"

"Goddamn!" John stared. "Come on. You're kidding. That's hard to believe. He's never told me anything about that. She must be out of her mind."

"That's exactly what I thought. But she swears it's true. I said it's probably hypnotism or something. Or low lights. But she said no, it was all done in broad daylight without any apparent tricks."

"I'll be damned," John said. "But then, I suppose it's possible. Do you think it is?"

I shrugged my shoulders. I told John that I studied a report by the nineteenth century American psychologist, William James, brother of the novelist Henry James.

"Don't tell me any more!" John interrupted facetiously. "Anyone whose brother is a novelist has to be suspect to begin with."

"Maybe so, but it seems that James had also gone to Scotland, to investigate a chemistry professor at a university over there, in Glasgow, who was said to practice levitation. James was skeptical at first, but was dumbfounded when this chemistry prof proceeded to demonstrate his powers. The guy laid himself out horizontally on a lab table, then raised his whole body up about twelve inches into the air. He then made his body move slowly across the room, about four feet above the floor, in this same horizontal position, with his hands and arms tight at his sides. It was a warm day, and all the windows were open. This guy floats right out through one of the windows, and it's three or four stories down to the courtyard below, but he floats right back in through another open window. When he's back to his original position above the lab table, he lowers himself slowly down, then sits up."

"That's unbelievable!" John said.

"Sure, and that's exactly how I felt about Jean's story of Ed levitating. Somehow, I don't think I'm ever going to ask Ed to demonstrate for me. If he actually did it, I'm not sure whether I could take it. I prefer to think Jean was hallucinating."

"Yeah." John rubbed his jaw uncomfortably. In the last few days he'd sprouted a heavy shadow of beard. "God, I need a shave. I didn't bring a toothbrush or a safety razor. But I've brought along this new plaything. Something brand new. It's an *electric* razor. It works great if you shave every day and don't let your beard grow too long," John laughed ruefully. "But so far, on this trip, I haven't found any electric outlets for it."

John said that he and Ed had also been discussing a new theory on different levels in writing, more or less based on Dr. Carl Jung's current psychological theories. We'd all been reading and mulling over Jung's newest book, *Modern Man in Search of a Soul*, which had been loaned to us by one of Jung's own pupils, Dr. Evelyn Ott. She was an attractive, forty-ish psychiatrist from Carmel, who had joined the Lab Group recently. We all admired her very much. She was slender and fashionable, with large luminous eyes and a gentle manner. We thought her extremely intelligent and aristocratic, and when she said anything we all listened carefully, which was rather unusual for that ordinarily noisy and argumentative bunch.

According to Jung's book, there were three levels, or plateaus, of consciousness to go through in the lifelong

Sketches of Marine Life in Cal Tech Lab Tanks Corona Del Mar 1936

Moray Eel

Sea Cucumber

development of the average individual. Each person shifts, more or less unpredictably, through these three stages, from the Naive, to the Sophisticated, and with luck, to the ultimate Conscious level of existence.

Emergence from the first Naive state (into which, like original sin, we all seem to be born) usually happens in late adolescence. By that time, it has become painfully obvious to most young people that their childish attitudes won't solve adult problems. They must fight their way up onto a more sophisticated level, where they generally remain for the rest of their lives. They find it a plateau where they can operate successfully, if they don't run into too many major problems.

Emergence from the Sophisticated level is far more difficult, Jung said, and usually occurs only in cases of emotional disaster—such as the loss of a loved one or a failure in a life-long business, or the breakup of a marriage. These psychic crash victims discover their sophisticated attitudes won't solve their big problems, either. If they survive a major psychic trauma, such as a nervous breakdown, they sometimes emerge to the Conscious level—a sort of psychological nirvana where there's enough peace to recover a perspective on life. As in the Air Corps, they've earned their wings the hard way. And it's a level that's not easy to maintain. Many people slide back into their earlier levels, but if they can stay up

4:30 Santa Barbara

there, they're recognized by their friends as superior—as leaders, gurus, even god-like personalities. Those of us who read the book agreed that the only people we knew personally who fit into this rarified Conscious classification were Ed and Evelyn Ott.

They were the Ying and the Yang of our little group. Ed was deeply impressed by her quiet wisdom and by her Jungian approach to life. As was John, at first through Ed's recycling of her ideas, and later through his own conversations with her as he got to know her better at the Lab.

Evelyn told us that when she informed Jung that she and Dr. Ott, another of his American pupils, were going to marry, he strongly advised against it. He warned them that they were incompatible types. But they were in love, and of course they ignored his advice—to their later sorrow, Evelyn said. After the birth of a son, Peter, they were divorced. Evelyn came back to the States with her child and opened a successful practice in Carmel.

Ed told us he considered himself a "reconstructed personality." At one period in his life, he hit bottom very hard, but he picked up the pieces, put them back together, and went on with his life. We understood he'd been divorced shortly before we met him, sometime in 1934, but he never talked about it. We presumed the trouble he referred to had been the breakup of his marriage.

His wife Nan came to the Lab once when there was a gathering of his friends. I opened the door and she asked to see Ed. She was an intense, dark-haired woman, quiet and self-contained. She talked briefly with Ed, in a very low voice—there was some problem with one of their three kids—then left unobtrusively. Ed rejoined the group, but offered no explanations. As always, he seemed imperturbable. He gave his advice, in a concerned and kindly manner, and that, apparently, was all she wanted.

If Ed fit Jung's definition of a Conscious personality, John certainly didn't. Because of his rather coarse and generally unkempt appearance, I'm sure no one had ever accused John of being an esthete. He wanted it that way. He deliberately played down anything that might be construed as "arty" in his own makeup.

He wore old workman's clothes, went unshaven for days, and *slouched* a lot. He enjoyed telling me that story about Howie Edminster, who said "I like to stink" so much that I figured John wished he had said it. Of course, his more sensitive writings indicated he had an inner core of spirituality, but he successfully disguised it, at least to the casual observer. Ed had frequently tried to excuse John's boorishness, and at times, his almost anthropoidal behavior, by saying indulgently—and rather enigmatically—"John is a much greater man than he is."

As we rode down the long grade into Santo Tomas valley that morning, with our boots propped up on our blanket rolls in front of us, John was trying to explain how Ed said he could apply Jung's theory of levels to his creative writing. The superficial plot of a novel, for example would correspond to the Naive level. A good yarn was entertainment, and universally accepted as such. The

Sophisticated level would be the characterization—of the protagonist and his associates—and would also appeal to almost everyone from the point of view of human interest, or gossip, if you will. The Conscious level would be the deeper meaning, or moral, of the story which most readers would only catch by implication. It would be an interesting challenge, for both the reader and the writer to keep up with each other as they unpeeled the levels back into the unknown—into the dim areas of racial memory and the ancient and forgotten symbolisms of the unconscious.

At the foot of the hill Ed turned the big Packard off the road and into a long, narrow yard lined with dusty open sheds.

"This must be he winery," John decided. "Ed said he always stops here."

We all got out to stretch our legs and inspect the little collection of buildings.

"Jean, you'll have to learn to drink wine," Ed was saying. "It's an acquired taste, like the strong, smelly cheese you've learned to like. And it's the only liquid that's really safe to drink down here."

Several vintners came out to the car to shake Ed's hand. They obviously remembered him well from previous trips. We went into their big, open, thatched shed to inspect the half dozen or so massive wooden wine casks, each one marked "5000 Gal." I made a quick sketch while one vintner drained the dark red wine into a ceramic pitcher, then filled up eight or ten long-necked bottles for us. Ed paid for the wine and we stored it carefully under Toby and the bed rolls.

An older winemaker came over to talk to Ed. He waved his hands and talked in rapid Spanish.

"What's he saying?" Jean asked.

"This is the guy who usually sells Ed the good strong goat cheese," John said. "Ed's always talking about it, you know. Says they bury it for him a whole year in the manure pile to give it a delicate flavor. I think they've had some trouble this year, though. I catch the words *queso*, *cabra*, and *tigre*. I think there's no cheese because the tigers have eaten the goats."

The Tortilla Maker — Ensenada

"No, that can't be it," Ed said. "They don't have tigers in Baja. Maybe a few wild cats. Or possibly a jaguar? I think the old boy wants us to follow him somewhere."

The old vintner led us around to the back of the wine shed, where there was a manure pile the size of a small haystack. He took a broken, rusty shovel and dug out a jute sack. Out of the sack he unwrapped a stained cardboard box of what was obviously American supermarket processed cheese in a five pound block. I could still read some of the big blue brand letters on the stained box.

Ed looked nonplussed. It wasn't what he wanted at all, but the old man had probably sent all the way to San Diego for the stuff—maybe made the long trip himself—just to bury it in the manure pile for Ed's next visit.

This was obviously a difficult problem in international diplomacy. If Ed said he didn't want it, the old man would be insulted. All that work for nothing! Ed dug out some dollar bills, and accepted the battered box of cheese graciously. We drove away in the car, but as soon as we were out of sight of the winery, Jean, John, and I burst into howls of laughter at Ed's expense.

"The look on your face!" Jean chortled. "That was priceless!"

Unlike John, who was a bit stuffy about his own image and was always trying to save face, Ed could laugh at himself. He appeared to enjoy the joke on him as much as we did—even though he was stuck with a big block of "imported" cheese he didn't want.

Whatever became of that cheese? I don't recall eating any of it, so I presume Ed threw it out the window somewhere along the way.

We pulled into the quaint little village of Santo Tomas. It seemed to be deserted. Siesta time, Ed said. He stopped the car at a one-pump gas station.

"I'd better fill up here," he told us. "It's the last place we can get decent gasoline. After this, we'll have to use the gas we brought along in tins. By the way, there's also two nice restrooms around in back, with Stateside plumbing. The last outpost of civilization, you know."

Ed watched as a young boy filled his tank, grinding away vigorously at an old-fashioned, vertical, gear-bar hand pump. John and I went around to the neat restroom in back. It was next to the town schoolhouse and we could hear the schoolkids' voices droning away in Spanish next door.

John pointed to a neat sign over the latrine and translated it for me:

> Protect your wife and friends. Visit the
> Federal Venereal Clinic once a week.

"The Mexicans are better off for medical services than we are," John noted. "And they're more liberal in their attitudes on morality, too. The word amigos means both your men and women friends!"

After the big Packard was gassed up, the four of us pitched in and washed it down, scraping off all the caked dust from the Baja back country. Then Ed pulled out of the gas station and we parked on the deserted street while I sketched the main intersection. John was particularly amused by a sign on one of the small thatched buildings that said *"TENDAJON."*

"*Tienda* means store," John chuckled. "So *Tendajon* must be giant store, or enormous store. That's pretty funny, when that whole building can't be more than twelve feet square."

"Let's go in," Jean said. "Maybe they're having a gigantic sale."

When we pushed into the building a tinny-sounding bell rang above the door. The store was clean and whitewashed but the shelves were pitifully understocked. A few cans of beans and peaches and a few boxes of soap were all that was available. Ed finally found something that interested him. In a glass case on top of the counter was a large coil of rope tobacco.

"Italian Toscani!" Ed exclaimed. "It's terribly strong, but it's good heady stuff."

"It looks like one of those rattlesnakes in your Lab." Jean was scornful about it. "Probably just as deadly, too. If you smoke it within a mile of me, I'll probably throw up again."

In his faltering Spanish, Ed began to dicker with the mustachioed proprietor. He was a small, dark-complexioned man, wearing a black suit with tight trousers and a vest over a white shirt with black arm bands, but without the suit coat. He became involved with Ed in a very serious discussion of measurements, done mostly by sign language, over the lengths of two cigars to be cut from the rope. They finally agreed on a length of eight inches or so, and the grocer whopped them off the rattlesnake with a meat cleaver, in two quick chops.

Ed held out a handful of American coins and the proprietor selected the ones he wanted. He then proceeded to wrap the two cigars in twists of newspaper. John and I had been standing behind Ed and Jean, watching the transaction with amusement, looking over their shoulders. Suddenly John nudged me in the ribs.

I looked at him questioningly. He nodded his head sideways and I looked around me. The store was rapidly filling up with townspeople, and they all seemed to be staring at us. I thought the siesta time must be over and they just came in to do their shopping, but John nudged me again and I looked more closely.

The men surrounding us in the store all looked as though they'd been hastily awakened from their siestas by some community alarm system, and had crammed on their clothes in a great hurry. They all seemed to be staring at Jean.

In spite of the heat, the women crowding into the store were wearing their customary long dark dresses and were wrapped to the teeth in heavy black shawls. They all seemed to be glaring at their men. What the hell was going on? I glanced at Jean and the light suddenly dawned.

Jean was unselfconsciously laughing and bantering with Ed over his purchase of the cigars, but, in her abbreviated red sunsuit, she must have appeared practically naked to these provincials. She was a head taller than the men and two heads taller than the women. The word must have gone around town to the men that there was a crazy Gringo girl in the store without any clothes on. They all had hurried in to check out the rumor, and their women had obviously rushed in after them. Perhaps they hoped to protect them from such a demoralizing sight?

"For Christ's sake," John said in a low voice. "Let's get Jean out of here before there's a riot!"

John took Ed by the elbow and I took Jean the same way. We ushered them out through the silent crowd as quickly as we could, with Jean protesting that she really hadn't finished shopping yet.

Ed Ricketts Baja 1936

"What's going on?" Ed asked when we reached the street outside.

"Never mind," John hissed dramatically. "Let's just get in the car and get to hell out of here."

We drove quickly out of Santo Tomas, past the little mob of townspeople who filed out of the "Enormous Store" to stare impassively after us. John cranked down the chauffeur's window and tried to explain what he felt about the scene we just left. Jean, of course, thought he was talking nonsense and just imagining things.

"No, Jean," I said. "I think John was right about it."

"Funny," Ed said. "I usually pick up things like that right away. I guess I was so busy buying the cigars that I didn't notice. Though, now that I think of it, on the way out I did sense something sinister about that crowd of people that seemed to have materialized out of nowhere."

John and Ed unwrapped their Toscani cigars and lit up, while Jean held her nose and I rolled down all the windows.

At the next little town we came to—I've forgotten the name, but I think it also sounded like San Fiasco—we didn't get out. Ed parked under the shade of a big tree while I sketched an amusing scene of an old 1922 Studebaker open touring car full of kids. John counted nine of them in the family. They were waiting patiently in the hot sun while their father was trying to add another patch to a flat tire. A big mule, watching them from their yard, let out a fierce bray occasionally, as though he were giving them the horselaugh for their undependable means of transportation.

While I was sketching, we saw a good example of what Ed had meant about meat and sanitation in Mexico. The federal meat truck had just pulled up in front of the only substantial-looking building in town, a small hotel and bar. The truck was an antique chain-driven Packard truck. The split-open beeves were stacked in the hot sun, in the open low-bed of the truck and as soon as it stopped, they were surrounded by a horrible cloud of black blow flies.

The truckdriver, wearing his badge of office—a blood-stained long brown leather apron—came around the back of the vehicle to lower the tailgate. He hauled out one of the big beeves and wrestled it up on his shoulder. It seemed much bigger than he was, but he staggered off with it and disappeared through the swinging double doors of the hotel.

Ten seconds after he left, a pack of squat yellow mongrel dogs gathered at the tailgate. All the dogs in Baja looked like they came from the same litter. They appeared to have sprung from an unhappy liaison between an Airedale and a coyote. Their intention was obvious. They wanted one of those sides of beef.

The leader of the pack leapt up into the truck bed, clamped his teeth over the leg of the closest carcass, and worried it off onto the dust of the unpaved street. The other dogs instantly sunk their teeth into it, and, with amazing cooperation, began dragging it rapidly down the street.

At that moment the truckdriver emerged from the hotel. He let out a shout of anger that could be heard for a mile. As if by a prearranged signal, all the men in town rushed out of the buildings in pursuit of the disappearing beef. They shouted, threw sticks, and kicked the dogs until they were finally driven off. Then the townspeople helped the truckdriver shoulder the carcass. He staggered back to the truck, dumped it in the bed, and closed up the tailgate. He took an old rag and wiped superficially at the dirt that had adhered to the meat. Then he went around, climbed into the driver's seat, clashed the gears, and lurched off in a great cloud of dust and disappointed blow flies.

Somewhat earlier on the trip, I remember John delivering a serio-comic dissertation on how to control Baja dogs. He'd made several trips to Mexico before and obviously considered himself an expert in this matter. There was one potent Spanish expletive that subdued them instantly. The word was ¡Fuera! Loosely translated, John said it meant, "scram, goddammit, before I cut you in half!"

John explained that the word had to be said just right, with the upside down Spanish exclamation point implied at the front of the word, and the right side up one at the back. Any self respecting Mexican dog that heard this word, said in just this fashion, immediately took off and was never seen or heard from again. John assured us this was all very true.

I can't recall hearing any of the townspeople shouting ¡Fuera! as they chased away the pack of dusty dogs stealing the side of beef. And I never had the opportunity of trying out the word myself, but I'm pretty sure that, as John said, it would have a great effect on any dogs that could understand Spanish at all well.

The road now turned back toward the Pacific Ocean. Ed told us our next stop was to be the beach at San Antonio del Mar, and we eventually arrived there, late in the afternoon. We stopped off the road, near some sand dunes. He said this was as close as we could drive to the beach, which was several hundred yards away, over the horizon. While waiting for the low tides after sunset, we unpacked our gear and made camp.

There were boulders and driftwood everywhere. We made a circle of rocks and started a brisk campfire. We fried up the *chorizo* sausages and heated the tortillas by draping them over the circle of fire-warmed rocks. The sausages exuded a gruesome orange grease as they sputtered in the big hot frying pan, but I must say they tasted a lot better with the accompaniment of about six bottles of red wine. Each of us also had a large can of cold stewed tomatoes. Ed opened the cans with a lever can-opener, and we carefully drank the stuff, right out of the ragged edges of the tins. Jean refused the wine, but she said the tomatoes tasted wonderfully refreshing.

I made a quick sketch of John, unshaven, holding a can of tomatoes, and Ed was delighted with it. Really caught John, he said. Better than any photograph. In fact, he liked it so much that the following week, when we got back to Monterey, he had Russ Cummings make a copy of it and he sent a print to an editor friend at the *San Jose Mercury*. Before publishing it, the editor checked with Carol, who was in Los Gatos working on the Steinbecks new house. She was furious about it. She said she thought it was very demeaning, and absolutely refused to allow it to be published. She wrote me a nasty open post card, addressed to the Lab, and accused me of trying to get free publicity at John's expense. She could write some pretty salty prose when she wanted to. The protective mother tigress, herself.

Ed read her post card and became equally furious. I ignored it, but Ed fired off another open post card to Carol in a sizzling retaliation. He told her I had nothing to do with it, and that she was being too goddamn defensive and offensive to suit him. It all blew over eventually, but Carol never bothered to apologize. It would have been out of character for her if she had.

She must have thought enough of the drawing not to tear up the print, however. Some forty years later, long after she was divorced from John, she gave it to Joel Hedgepeth, who was doing some research on the Row. Hedgepeth asked me if he could publish it in his book, but I refused. I felt I'd like to save it for this book, if I ever got around to writing it. After we finished our leisurely camp supper on the dunes at San Antonio, John asked Ed how long before the tide would be out and we'd start collecting.

"A little more than an hour, I'd say," Ed replied, checking his wristwatch.

"Yeah? Well, look. I'd like to read you the last few chapters of my new book. Hold on a second." He walked over to the car and dug out the black ledger with the flattened roll of white proof sheets in it. By the time he returned, Ed had the Coleman lamps burning. We settled down around the campfire to listen to John's newest story.

"Back there at the Greenfield bridge," John began. "Remember, I showed you that spot by the river? That's where this incident happened. In fact, that's my title for the book—*A Thing That Happened*. Pat, my publisher, thinks *Something That Happened* is better, but that's still open to debate. Anyway, as I said, this book is more a play than a novel. I think it could go right on the stage, without any rewriting whatsoever."

John began to read the last chapters of the book which was to be published the following spring, under the title *Of Mice and Men*. He had a low, sonorous voice, a little husky because he smoked too much, but like most writers, I thought, he was too involved in his own work to be its best reader. The story had a fine feeling of western ranches and ranch hands, but John was so caught up in the lives of his characters that, towards the end, his voice broke with emotion. He read the last part about the shooting of Lennie with choking difficulty and the tears were brimming out of his eyes.

It had been a long day. I was full of hot, spicy food, and I'd put away two bottles of red wine. I'm afraid I dozed off here and there. When he finished, there was a long moment of impressive silence before Ed and Jean congratulated him. They said it was one of the best things he'd ever written.

"What do you think, Bruce?"

"Well," I rubbed my jaw, trying to think of something polite to say. "It's interesting, John, but I don't think it will sell."

John looked a little hurt, but didn't say anything. After all, in his career as a writer, he'd encountered a lot more severe criticism than that. Professional New York critics always seemed to have a field day picking his work to pieces, but I suppose he would have liked a little more support from a friend.

Of course, my verdict on *Mice and Men* was about as far from accurate as a guy could get. I'm sure it's sold better than anything else he ever wrote. It was a Book-of-the-Month Club selection and has been translated into dozens of languages around the world. It sold to Hollywood for a fine motion picture. With the aid of the New York director, George Kaufman, it was made into a great Broadway play that ran for over two hundred performances. It won the 1937-1938 New York Drama Critics' Circle Award almost unanimously—which indicated that John and the critics' mutual antagonism might be coming to an end.

Since then the play has been performed thousands of times in professional and amateur theaters everywhere. It's been done more than once on television, and made into an "interesting"—if not successful—opera in Seattle.

Although John himself said he was never satisfied with *Mice and Men*, the only excuse for my judgmental error, other than stupidity, might be that I was tired, sleepy, and in a slight stupor from too much food and wine. Some fifteen years later, at the Wharf Theater in Monterey, I realized what a fine vehicle the play was, when I played the big moron, Lennie, for which, because of the above gaffe, I was probably typecast. I found the role to be one of the most satisfying in my short career as an actor.

We collected late into the night in the shallow tide pools of the San Antonio del Mar beach. We gathered hundreds of chitons, a fist-sized mollusk, each with eight interlocking butterfly shells on its back. Ed said they were exactly what he wanted. We harvested I don't know how many gunny sacks full of them.

The following morning Ed was up early setting out the chitons in shallow trays and pouring liquid over them. I made a quick sketch of Ed, John, and the chitons and labeled it, in my bastard Spanish, *Los Scientistos*, though I should have remembered from my school Spanish that the right word was *cientificos*.

"Chitons look a lot like lobster tails," I said somewhat hungrily. "Do you think they're good to eat?"

"I don't know," Ed said. "I hadn't thought about it. They're mollusks. The same family as abalone, and I'm sure the Indians ate them. The Indians had teeth and jaws like iron. They ate abalone without pounding them beforehand."

"Old Pop Ernst, the restaurateur down on the Monterey wharf," John said, "is supposed to get the credit for discovering that prepounding made them into a delicacy."

"If he did," Ed replied, "He'll also probably get the credit for their extinction. The commercial divers are taking them by the ton nowadays. Every vacant lot in Monterey is a dumping ground for empty shells. The Chinese used to use the shells for jewelry. Mother of Pearl. But they don't do that anymore. I guess there's too many of them lying around."

"I heard a story about one of the early Chinese squatters on China Point," I said. "He tried to pry an abalone off the rocks at low tide by using his fingers. The abalone clamped down on them, and he couldn't get free. The tide came in and drowned him. I guess that's why they always say to use a tire iron to get them off."

I finished my sketch, and I strolled with him over the dunes to see how the beach looked in the daytime. It was an overcast morning and we were amazed to see the beach was all black sand, stretching off ominously north and south and disappearing into the mists. It had an eerie, primordial quality, like an ancient silurian seascape when the first scorpion land life had crawled out of the sea.

"This place gives me the willies," John said. "Let's get out of here."

Jim Fitzgerald

We went back over the dunes to our camp where, surprisingly, the sun was shining very brightly. In superstitious tones John described the black beach to Ed, who was still working on the chitons, and to Jean, who had just got up and was starting breakfast. Suddenly she let out a cry of surprise and anger.

"John! What are you doing?"

"Huh? I'm brushing my teeth."

"But that's my toothbrush!"

"Sure. I forgot mine. I'm fastidious. And you've got such nice-looking teeth I borrow yours, rather than Ed's or Bruce's."

"Damn you! That's disgusting," Jean sputtered. "I wondered why my toothbrush was always so soggy in the mornings! That's really an outrage! A toothbrush is a very private machine, for God's sake! Couldn't you have used your finger, or some sagebrush, or a piece of cactus, or something?"

"Aw, come on, Jean," John said placatingly. "I haven't poisoned you yet, have I?"

"How do I know? It's just the idea of it." Jean scowled fiercely at him. "I can't believe anyone would do such a thing! Good God! That's unforgivable! I'm going over to that black beach and soak my toothbrush in salt water for half an hour. And I'll take a nice long bath, too, while I'm at it."

We watched her with amusement as she stalked off over the dunes toward the ocean, clutching a bar of soap, a towel, and the desecrated toothbrush against her red sunsuit.

"She's got a wonderful temper," John conceded with his wide grin. "Almost as bad as Carol's."

Ed smiled and went back to work processing the chitons. He said he was extremely delighted with the large haul we made.

"Bruce, you asked whether these things were edible. While you and John were gone, I thought I'd try to eat one, but then I changed my mind. I said to myself, why should I? If they are edible, it might lead to another of man's inroads on nature's food sources. Unrestricted harvesting.

Another classic crime against a species. In the last few generations we've wiped out the passenger pigeon, the dodo bird, the buffalo, the sea otter, and Stellar's sea cow, to name just a few. The Monterey sardine will be next, believe me. They're burning them on the Row for fertilizer meal these days. More profitable than canning them for human consumption. I understand the boats even hold back a day or so longer from port, so they'll be too soft for canning. I've warned them, but it doesn't do any good. The big cannery head-men just laugh and say there's more fish in the sea than ever came out of it."

"Do you think they can wipe out the sardines?" I asked doubtfully. "There's billions of them. Some of the boats catch so many that the fish spill out of the holds, over the decks, and into the cabins, too. They've even overloaded the boats so much that some of them have foundered and gone under."

"Sure," Ed agreed. "There's lots of them now, but the big purse nets are breaking up the schools into such small groups they can't reproduce. Like gregarious herds of land animals, the sardines depend on their great numbers for safety and reproduction. In 1911, for example, the Portuguese suddenly discovered they fished out all their local sardines. Their big canning industry collapsed. Now they go all the way to the New England Grand Banks after fish."

"I wonder what's keeping Jean," I said, checking my wristwatch. "She should have been back by now."

"It'll probably take her a long while to cool off," John snickered, remembering her violent outburst. "How about borrowing your toothbrush tomorrow, Ed?"

"We'll be back in San Diego in a couple days," Ed said. "You can buy a new one, for God's sake."

"Hey, look!" I pointed to the horizon. "There she comes. Over there."

Jean was striding rapidly over the dunes towards us. As she approached, we noticed she looked flustered. Her cheeks were as bright red as her sunsuit.

"What happened?" Ed asked in sudden concern.

"The darndest thing," Jean answered with an embarrassed laugh. "You won't believe it! When I got over there to that great black empty beach—it was just as John and Bruce described—except the sun had broken through the clouds and it wasn't ominous at all. It was beautiful! It wasn't a bit sinister. I stripped and put my suit and towel on the dry sand. The beach is so gradual I had to walk out a hundred feet or more, and still the water only came up to my ankles. I thought, for Pete's sake, I'll have to walk half was to China to get a decent bath, so I gave up and started to soap myself down.

"I heard something and looked up to see these two horsemen, riding hell-for-leather, right down the beach toward me. What could I do? I was too far away from my clothes and my towel. The water was too shallow to sit down in, let alone hide. I just stood there in a half crouch, with my mouth open, like the girl in that stupid *September Morn* painting.

"They were bearing right down on me, with their horses' hooves splashing up great clouds of spray. I could see these two men were really villainous looking cusses, too. Unshaven, black week-old growths of beard. I realized you three couldn't hear me, way over here, even if I screamed my bloody head off. So I just stood my ground and watched them come at me. I had fleeting thoughts that I'd be kidnapped, or killed, or raped, or something, and there wasn't much I could do about it. But they pounded right on by me without slowing down one bit! Splashed me all over with the spray. And one of them looked back at me over his shoulder, his eyes rolling in his head, and crossed himself! Can you beat that?" Jean shook her head and laughed somewhat shakily.

"On that black, uninhabited lonely beach, where they'd probably never seen anyone before, they must have thought I was an apparition, or an incubus, or a succubus, or whatever those old monks in the Middle Ages called the night witches they claimed were always trying to seduce them"

"Succubi," John said. "I think the incubi were the male demons that were always trying to screw the nuns. The medieval church even recognized their existence by law, if you can believe that."

"Are you sure you're all right?" I asked Jean.

"Sure, I'm fine. Just scared the hell out of me, that's all. And I was embarrassed to tears. Wasn't that a crazy experience? But it turned out all right. I'm hungry. What are we having for breakfast?"

"More chorizos and tortillas," Ed said. "We'll have to finish them up, even if we can't stand them. But, at least, there's three bottles of wine left to put the fire out with."

"You three can eat the chorizos," Jean decided. "It was all I could do to keep them down last night. I'll just have tortillas and coffee, thank you." We finished our breakfast and started to break camp. Ed was still trying to make up his mind whether to go on farther south.

"There's a fine beach at San Quentin," he told us. "But we made such a good haul last night, we're really loaded down."

While he was thinking about it, the Mexican government mail truck drove up. It was a battered Model A wooden station wagon, covered with dried mud and dust. The two mailmen spoke fairly good English and Ed pumped them about the condition of the road farther on south.

They grinned and shook their heads, making derogatory gestures with their hands.

"*Espantoso!* Pretty damn Gods-awful." They pointed to the inside of their station wagon which seemed to be filled more with shovels, bars, chains, and blocks and tackle then it was with mail. They told us they made the trip all the way down to San Jose del Cabo, on the tip of Baja, once a week, year round, and they always prayed a lot. They waved good-bye and lurched away in their sturdy old Ford, followed by a huge cloud of dust.

That conversation decided Ed to turn back. We tightened down all the gear. Ed started the motor to let it warm up. While we were waiting, we noticed a small, solitary figure approaching us inland from the hills. He seemed to be heading directly toward us. We waited for him with idle curiosity.

He was an odd, rotund, little man of indiscriminate age, perhaps in his fifties or sixties. He was dapper and well-dressed in a fine gray cloth suit with a red cummerbund sash. He wore a wide-brimmed Catalan hat and looked like a misplaced *boulevardier* from Mexico City. We couldn't imagine what he was doing strolling towards us in that wilderness country.

He took off his hat and nodded to us very formally. His hair was gray and his skin was sun-tanned, but we could see that he had basically a Yankee complexion. He didn't say a word. He put his hat back on and stood there staring at us. There was something quaint and old-fashioned about him that reminded me of a Tenielle woodblock

illustration of Tweedldee in an old copy of *Alice in Wonderland*.

We all got out and tried talking to him in English and our broken Spanish. He smiled and nodded, but didn't answer. Perhaps he was deaf and dumb? He seemed particularly interested in watching Jean in her sunsuit and big Mexican straw hat. After a bit he took off his hat and bowed again. Then he put his hat back on, turned on his heel like a soldier, and walked away back up into the hills from where he came.

"Now, what in hell do you make of that?" I asked, scratching my jaw.

"I can't imagine." Ed was equally baffled.

Jean said, "Now, that was certainly a strange little man!"

"There's got to be a story in this," John said. His fiction writing faculties were beginning to whir. "I noticed something when we were driving along back there, late yesterday afternoon. There was a dusty old sign pointing up a narrow road into the hills that said, "Johnson Ranch." You know what I think? That was old man Johnson, himself. Probably from an expatriate family that's lived down here for generations. Americans, or maybe Swedes, originally. Lived so long in these boondocks, they've forgotten how to talk in any language. So those horsemen who saw Jean brass naked on the beach this morning are a couple of Johnson Ranch riders. They gallop back to their *patron*, tell him all about this beautiful nymph that's come up out of the sea. So he gets all dressed up to come down to introduce himself to her, but he discovers we're just a bunch of scruffy gringos, so he turns right around and goes back home again. How's that?"

"As good a guess as any," Ed said.

"Sounds all right to me," I agreed. "Write it up and I'll print it."

"Sounds like nonsense," Jean decided. "I'm sure there's a better explanation, but I can't imagine what it is."

We climbed back into the big Packard, Ed put the car in gear, and we started north. The trip back to Monterey was

Jean doing "Mexican Hat Dance" act at a Tia Juana Shop. Baja, 1936

long, straight-through, and uninterrupted driving. Ed was indefatigable. It was a much different trip than the one on the way down. There was no stopping at beaches, no small adventures, almost no conversation. Jean, John, me, and the dog dozed most of the time while Ed drove on relentlessly. We reached San Diego by nightfall and checked into a nondescript motor court.

Motor courts, during the Depression, all looked alike. There were no fancy swimming pools or restaurants connected to them. They were just rows of little 10 x 12 chickenshed wooden shacks, with a covered space between them to park a car. They usually had one or two uncomfortable iron double beds in them, a minimum of plumbing, and sometimes a small sink and a hot plate in one corner to serve as a kitchen.

Spartan accommodations, but for a couple bucks a night, they were more than adequate, and what we were used to in those times. They all seemed to be painted gray on the outside and cream-colored on the inside. The one we stopped at in San Diego had separate shower bathhouses, one for men and one for women, next to the office cabin.

Jean went into hers and we three men went into ours. It was one big room with a cement floor, no partitions, and a dozen shower heads. But it was great. The water was hot and steaming, there was lots of soap, and it felt like we washed away ten pounds apiece of Baja dust.

The following morning we hit the road early, bound north for Monterey. Ed was anxious to get his precious cargo back to the Lab as soon as possible for processing. He didn't seem to mind at all when the rest of us dozed through the whole trip home. We were trying to catch up on a week of lost sleep.

Jean, John, his dog Toby, and I all continued to sleep

Jean Cat-Napping at the Lighthouse   1936 Ensenada
Bruce Ariss

like big lumps. I don't recall stopping once, even for coffee, sandwiches, or gas, though I suppose we did. We arrived back in Monterey about dusk of that same long day. The canneries on the Row hulked dark and empty against the late evening sky. Everything seemed just as we left it some half dozen days ago, but on the way through town, we'd seen sobering newspaper headlines:

MUSSOLINI INVADES ETHIOPIA

We were too tired to think about it. Ed told us to forget trying to help him unpack. He'd take care of all that. Jean and I started up our old Dodge touring car in the Lab basement and drove John home. We dropped him and his dog off at Eleventh Street and went on to our own little cabin under the tall pines on Ninth.

The note we pinned to our door before we left was still there. It was a note for an artist friend from San Francisco, whom we thought might visit us that week:

WARREN
GONE TO MEXICO
BACK SOON.
           Bruce & Jean

Obviously Warren hadn't made it, which was rather too bad, because if he had, he might have turned off the garden hose which I apparently left running in the flower box. When Jean snapped on the yard light I could see there was water all over the place.

It could have been worse. We could have been away for a month. We'd only been away for a week—actually one day short of a week—but, as in Thoreau's *A Week on the Concord and Merrimack Rivers*, the journey had been crammed full of so much, so many incidents and accidents, that it seemed we had been away for a month. I smiled to myself, trying to recall that amusing story of Thoreau's book. It hadn't sold worth a damn, and he bought all the remainders from his publisher for a few cents on the dollar. He built shelves and put the books all around in his little cabin on Walden Pond. Then he proudly recorded in his journal that he had hundreds of books in his library, every one of which he wrote himself.

I was too tired to do anything about draining away the water in the yard. I shut off the faucet and the light, said to hell with it, and followed Jean into bed.

Jean posed as a girl in cannery worker's garb. The dark building directly across the street is Flora Woods' notorious brothel, The Lone Star "Restaurant." (Dora Flood's Bear Flag sporting house, in Steinbeck's Cannery Row.) The Old Blue Diner canteen bus was parked, during the sardine canning season, in front of the "vacant" lot which held the big rusty boilers used as housing by some of the bums on the Row. The "Palace Flop House" was just behind the boilers, and on the other side of the railroad tracks. Wing Chong's "glorious" grocery store (Lee Chong's in the book).

SECTION III

CANNERY ROW REVISITED

IT WAS AFTER SUNDOWN on a Saturday night, early in August of 1936. The Monterey sardine fishing and canning season had officially opened and the Row was pulsing with its usual madhouse din. All the big canneries were in violent action, grinding, steaming, and clanking. Hulking drayage trucks, bellowing their air horns, shouldered their way through the mess of automobile and foot traffic on the narrow street. The odor of steaming or burning sardines was overpowering.

Beyond the dark barrier of the bulky waterfront buildings, from out on the black waters of the bay, came the shouts and curses of the fishermen on their flood-lit boats. Some of them were still unloading the silvery catches into the floating offshore storage hoppers. Often there were so many purse seiner fishing boats in the harbor at sunset getting ready to sail, it seemed possible that one could walk across the harbor, from boat to boat, and reach the breakwater a mile or so across the bay to the other side of the anchorages. In earlier times they used the scooping brail nets, but this method had proved too slow, and now the nine inch fish were usually pumped through ten inch black rubber hoses, underwater, directly from the boats' holds into the canneries. The fish were then transported up fish ladder chains into the stilt-legged weighing towers. After they were credited to the boat, the weighmaster dumped them down a chute and gravity took them to the workers lined up at the cutting chains. The chains carried the sardines along until their heads and tails were lopped off so they could fit into the oval cans.

All the large-scale purse seine fishing was done at night, in the "dark of the moon," because the huge schools could only be seen in pitch dark when they created a luminous glow while feeding on their diet of single-celled plankton. When a school was sighted, the purse seiner idled its big diesel engine, turned off its lights, and absolute quiet was maintained. A skiff was lowered with two men in it who fastened one end of the long net to the skiff while the purse seiner quietly circled the entire school until it was back again to the skiff. A sudden noise or a light could frighten the school away and ruin the set.

The nets were enormous and very expensive. They cost over $10,000 and were almost a quarter of a mile long. They were more than two hundred feet deep, with floats at the top and metal weights and rings at the bottom. Once the school was encircled by this long wall, a rope running through the bottom rings was slowly cinched up to enclose the complete school of sardines. Then the motor and the lights were turned up and the big net was cinched in, loop by loop, to spill the still struggling fish into the empty hold. If the school was larger than the boat could handle, others were called in by ship's radio to share the surplus.

If the fleet was lucky enough to find fish in relatively close waters, it would be back in Monterey, off-loading at the canneries, before dawn. The cannery workers would then take over on the canning, packing, and reducing. As mass fishing continued to develop into the war years, the fleet was obliged to cruise farther and farther from Monterey to locate the larger schools.

Mass sardine fishing out of Monterey was cold, dark, and dangerous work. Not infrequently a fisherman accidentally went over the side into the night waters and was lost. A few days later there would be a solemn and emotional Sicillian memorial service held in the ancient adobe Catholic chapel in Monterey.

On each big purse seiner there was generally a crew of eight to twelve men. The smaller, clipper-bowed half ringers worked with a half dozen men at the nets. Line or market fishermen usually worked in pairs, or even, occasionally, alone in their smaller boats.

Wartime shortages increased the demand for sardines because they were an inexpensive and easily shipped protein. The Monterey fleet and the canneries enlarged tenfold to fill the need. The average yearly catch was running about a quarter of a million tons. Boats increased in size until they were over a hundred feet long. More blocks of canneries were built along the waterfront.

The most profitable operation was in the reduction plants. Fish refuse and sardines too soft to can were squeezed flat for their oil, which was used commercially in paint, linoleum, and so on. The residue was burned in heated, awful-smelling, rotating, gigantic cylinders. This produced the fertilizer meal that was bagged and shipped to farmers around the country.

Ed Ricketts' unheeded warnings came true. After the war ended the sardines almost completely disappeared. "Where did they all go," the unemployed fishermen and canners asked incredulously.

"Into the cans," Ed answered.

Once, on an impulse, Ed drove a half dozen of us in his old Packard limousine up into the high and distant reaches of the Corral de Tierra. He said it looked like there was going to be a magnificent sunset. He wanted us to listen to a new record album he bought of Moussorgsky's *Night on Bald Mountain*. As the sun went down he ceremoniously played the thunderous music on a beat-up old hand-wound portable Victrola that he must have salvaged somewhere from a junk shop. The group of us stood there solemnly, silhouetted against the sky at the top of the grade, like mourners in an immense cathedral, watching the great orange oblate sun go down to the scratchy and thunderous sounds of that immortal music.

John was never as fascinated by fine music as Ed. Whenever he could make time from his laboratory work, the older man loved to play his recordings of early church Gregorian Chants, his Mozart, and his Bach. The rest of us would often lounge around in the dim-lit upstairs, drinking red wine and "helping Ed listen."

John was too restless to stay long at these sessions. He would get up, grin and wave, and slip away unobtrusively to walk past the Boatworks on China Point along the dozen blocks to his home on Eleventh Street. John had commissioned Pol Verbeck to build him another fine phonograph like Ed's. Perhaps he preferred to listen to music alone, but, more likely, he was returning to his writing, which had always been the most important muse for John.

The only piece of music I ever recall John becoming excited about was a frothy bit by the contemporary French composer, Jacques Ibert. John had a record of his *Divertissement,* an amusing lampoon of the heavy European symphonies and operas of the past century. John played this over and over on Ed's machine, laughing uproariously and trying to get us all to enjoy it as much as he did.

One particular 1936 prewar Saturday night Ed was downstairs in the basement of his little laboratory, working late, by himself, as he often did. He had kept himself busy for the last several months, processing all the stuff we collected in Baja, filing it on his basement shelves, filling all his back orders.

Jean and I sat at the windows upstairs in the darkened Lab, talking and idly watching the patrons of Flora's place, across the street, moving in and out of the big door. On either side of it, standing at attention on the porch, was an army MP in full regalia, with rifle at parade rest. It was a warm night and those MPs must have been hot and uncomfortable, but they were on duty and stared straight ahead unblinking.

By their very presence on the whorehouse porch the two official-looking MPs seemed to give legitimate business status to Flora's establishment. We thought we knew why they were there. A week before, one of the cavalrymen from the post had gone berserk and pretty well wrecked the joint. The two armed guards were obviously the presidio commandant's answer to Flora's shrill complaints over the incident.

As it happened, we also knew the cavalryman who'd caused all the trouble. He was a swarthy muscular, and hard-bitten Oklahoman named Billy Thatcher. He was half Cherokee, and wholly nuts on paydays when he had a few drinks under his belt. Sober, Billy was so polite it was painful.

He was full of wild yarns about his adventures that seemed to be the product of an inflamed imagination. Yet he told them with such honest sincerity they must have had a kernel of truth to them. For example, sitting around in the dusk one evening at the Lab, he told this fantastic story that happened to him when he was a deck hand on an old tramp steamer in the South Pacific.

He told us the old tub had just weathered a frightful typhoon, and the ship was wallowing in the quiet waters of the typhoon's "eye." The center of a typhoon is completely calm, Billy explained, but the crew knew they would soon hit the other side and were battening everything down for the expected new blow. Just then someone shouted "Man Overboard."

The crew members rushed to the rail and saw a naked man swimming slowly in the glassy sea. They threw him a rope. He climbed right up it, as nimbly as an acrobat, and stood on the deck in front of them. He was the strangest-looking man they'd ever seen. He was of medium height and very heavily muscled, but his skin was of an unusual greenish cast. He had folds of skin in his throat, like gills, and his feet and hands were *webbed*. He spoke to them in a musical language that no one understood.

Old Booth Cannery 1937

The sailors crowded around him with their mouths open in amazement. The big tough bosun came roaring up, shouting curses and driving the men back to their tasks. When he saw the stranger on his ship he thrust out his arm to knock him aside. The fishman caught his wrist in his webbed hands and squeezed, and the big bosun, screaming with pain, collapsed to the deck. Then the strange creature leaped gracefully up on to the taffrail and executed a perfect dive back into the sea.

Seconds later the typhoon cracked down on them again and they only had time to think about saving their ship. They never saw the fishman again.

When Billy finished telling this story, his voice was choked with awe at the memory, and his face was bathed in sweat. It was a hell of an impressive yarn, but I didn't believe one word of it. I figured he was probably sweating

SEALER

for fear someone would call him a damned liar. Nobody did, though I suspected they wanted to.

We told John this wild story later, and asked him what he thought about Jean or me writing it down for *Esquire* magazine. John agreed it was a good yarn, but almost too good. He figured Billy had probably read it in an old copy of *Weird Tales* or *Amazing Stories*, two popular magazines of the day. We'd very like turn out to be plagiarists if we used it. Some young writer had just recently done a rewrite of an Ambrose Bierce short story. It had been published in *Esquire* and hundreds of readers had written in about it.

So we forgot about that idea, but it wasn't so easy to forget about Billy. The following weekend after he'd told the story, Billy got drunk on payday, as usual. He dropped into Flora's place. He was teamed up with a cute little prostitute who was new to the place. She told Billy she was from his very own home town in Oklahoma and that, actually, she was a virgin who'd been kidnapped when she was an innocent high school girl and sold into white slavery. It was probably the same line she gave everyone, but Billy believed every word of it, just as he must have believed that his own unbelievable tales were true.

He went falling-down crazy with rage and tore the place to pieces. Threw chairs through mirrors and windows, and upended all the tables. He dragged the poor prostitute in her flimsy gown out into the street in the middle of the night, got her into a cab with him, and sped with her to the bus station. He bought her a one-way ticket to his home town in Oklahoma, shoved her on the outgoing bus, then tried to escape the MPs who were combing the countryside for him. They cornered him in the Hotel Del Monte train depot and there was a fabulous roaring scrap before they finally subdued him.

He then spent two or three weeks in the stockade. We heard it had taken that poor dazed prostitute almost that long to find out where she was, and then make her way back home again to Flora's place.

Business was so good at the Lone Star that Flora purchased a brand new seven-passenger shiny Buick sedan. There was no garage in her building so she asked Ed if she could rent his. Ed agreed. He could use the money, and there was no reason why his old Packard shouldn't sit out on the street. Nobody would bother it.

Every morning, for quite a time thereafter, the tall skinny handyman-chauffeur would bring over three or four of the girls to drive around shopping or to the beach.

They were mostly nice looking girls. For street wear they wore tailored suits, high heels, and silk stockings, and wore cute little hats with saucy bits of veil over their eyes. There was no way to tell them from any of the most dignified ladies of Monterey except, perhaps, that they were better dressed.

The girls were very grateful to Ed for his fatherly advice. Just how grateful we found out one day when a salesman from a rival medical supply house stopped in to see him. He asked Ed point blank where in hell he managed to get such an exclusive series of slides on the development of the human embryo. Ed just smiled and looked enigmatic. Jean and I glanced at each other and raised our eyebrows. Those gals must have showed their gratitude by saving all their miscarriages for him!

Ed also kept fetuses in advanced stages, in jars of alcohol, on his basement storage shelves. The alcohol gave them a greenish tinge. I thought they were fascinating, but rather repulsive rubbery-looking little creatures. They stared back at me like miniature versions of Billy Thatcher's weird deep sea denizen.

My designs for a big WPA mural had been approved and I ground the colors for it downstairs in Ed's laboratory ball mill. I had almost fifty quarts of different colors—lovely blues and greens and earth colors—all ground in distilled water in Ed's mill. I stored the jars of colors between Ed's jars of embryos. I thought their bright hues gave a nice feeling of warmth to the rather morgue-like atmosphere of the storeroom.

Ordinarily, Ed used the ball mill to grind what he called "mass"—a colored dye he infused into the various systems of his "crucified" cats—as Jean referred to them with distaste. Actually the cats were strays who were painlessly asphyxiated. They were captured for Ed by local urchins who received 25¢ apiece for them. If they appeared to be pet cats and not strays, Ed checked the Lost and Found columns and waited several weeks before doing away with them. He strapped the animals to cross-shaped wooden cradles while he ran the colors into them through needles and tubes. Red for the arterial system, blue for the venous system, yellow for the nervous system, and so on. These gaily colored little mummies were apparently quite in demand by medical and veterinarian schools.

About this time the *Monterey Trader*, a small weekly reform newspaper, published nearby on Lighthouse Avenue, started a campaign against Flora's place. They printed the license numbers of all cars parked in front of the whorehouse so their readers might know who Flora's patrons were. She tipped off her regular customers, of course, who then parked around the corner. Some of Ed's more conservative friends, doctors, lawyers, and professors (amazed to find all the empty parking spots in front of Flora's) parked there and came across to the Lab. They were embarrassed to find their licenses listed as Flora's patrons in the following editions of *The Trader*.

One of those unjustly caught in *The Trader's* net was Rube Tice, the big electrical contractor and inventor, who often dropped by Ed's place to unload his worries about his finances.

That afternoon he told Ed, "If I only had ten thousand bucks, right now, I could meet my payroll. Clean up everything nicely."

Ed said, "I could do likewise with a thousand."

And I said, "It's all relative. If I had a hundred, I'd be okay."

To top all this, as a further example of financial comparisons amongst the Lab Group, it was to be only a few years later that Steinbeck would need several hundred thousand dollars for a divorce settlement just to get out of his moribund marriage with his first wife, Carol.

For a short while, when we first met Ed, we were aware of a quiet older man who helped out occasionally in the basement lab. It was Ed's retired father who, in the years before his death, tried to help, but was terribly inept. Ed smiled indulgently.

"Most people, by the law of averages, will get 50 percent of their tasks done right. Not my dad. He gets 100 percent of everything he does wrong. That proves to me he's extraordinarily brilliant, because he must also know what's 100 percent right!"

At that time John Steinbeck had gone off to the Central Valley with a guy from the government's new sanitary labor camp setup. John was researching the deplorable conditions in the older private labor camps for a forthcoming series of exposé articles for a San Francisco newspaper. This research would prove to be crucial later for a "big novel" that was beginning to take form in his mind.

He and his companion had thrown together some camping gear and were traveling in an old second-hand '32 Ford delivery truck John had bought from a bakery. He called it his Pie Wagon—possibly referring to the popular

Pie in the Sky song of early labor organizers. We were under the distinct impression that John was then going to drive on by himself to Oklahoma. He planned to bum back along Highway 66, living with the disinherited dust bowl refugees that were then straggling into California by the thousands.

His "authorized" biographer, Jack Benson, stated that John never made that trip, and only implied to his friends that he had. Too bad. It made such a good, earthy comparison to his much later *Travels With Charley* tour which John made in a brand new camper, accompanied by his French poodle.

In Shakespeare's plays, a woman's pubic patch was referred to as a flag. I once asked John if he intended a hidden pun there—Bare Flag—the name of his Cannery Row whorehouse. As usual, when quizzed about his literary devices, John merely looked enigmatic and didn't answer the question.

Most of Steinbeck's literary characters seemed quite synthetic to me, perhaps because they were amalgamations of so many actual people he'd met, fused into one by creative coatings of words. A few, like "Doc" in *Cannery Row*, were more easily recognizable, though, as in Ed's case, the portrayal might not be at all three-dimensional. The character of "Mac," in the same book, was obviously inspired by Gabe, one of the locals on the Row. He was a part-time cannery worker and a full-time bum. Gabe lived in the "Palace Flop House," which was actually a one-story men's dormitory located on the west side of the S.P tracks, directly behind Flora's Lone Star Restaurant. When Gabe was unable to fast-talk a loan from Ed, he'd sometimes work for him.

One late-night incident happened which I think inspired the frog-hunt story in John's book. Gabe and his buddies had brought in a big haul from Carmel Valley—half a dozen pulsating, over-sized gunny sacks full of bull frogs. Each frog was as big as my hand, and they were all alive and extremely vocal. Ed said it was a windfall. John and I went down into the basement of the Lab to help him process them. There must have been at least a thousand of them. At the going price of a nickle apiece that Ed paid, I figured that Gabe and all his flophouse friends would be falling-down drunk for a month or more. Every six frogs meant a gallon of red wine!

The incident stood out in my mind mainly because one of the bullfrogs in the bunch was a mutant. When Ed picked up this big frog to anesthetize it, instead of a standard two-tone bellow, it let out a piercing scream. It sounded exactly like a woman being murdered. Ed dropped the frog and jumped back in surprise.

John and I were clinically fascinated by this anomaly. We thought it an example of one of those rare evolutionary deviations that play a part in natural selection. But Ed was quite unnerved by it. He said he couldn't take the screams. His hands were actually shaking when he turned the frog over to us to chloroform.

Later, after all the frogs were put to sleep, Ed refused to say why he was upset. I remember thinking that Ed might be taking too seriously some of those Eastern theories about the transmigration of the soul that he was reading late at night.

As I think about it now, some fifty years later, I find the incident unusual only in that Ed was the one disturbed by it, and not John, who was much more superstitious about such things.

Shortly after we returned from Baja, there was a banquet given, more or less in our honor, by Mrs. Hattie Gragg. Hattie was a marvelous old gal, a member of a pioneer society family, who held court in her venerable Stokes-Gragg Adobe (later, Gallatin's Restaurant) in downtown Monterey. Hattie was very fond of Jean.

At the banquet, Hattie sat Jean on her right with John and Ed on her left. I was seated next to Jean, with Gus and Marcelle Gay at my right. It was a memorable occasion, with some two dozen important town citizens in attendance. Hattie's dinners were famous. She served early Spanish California foods in a fabulous old-world surrounding.

The long table was covered with a priceless heirloom

In the 30s the Sardine Fleet made Monterey Bay a busy Working harbor

Spanish lace tablecloth and lit by a half dozen noble silver candelabras. The pièce de résistance was a giant tureen of garbanzos and tripe, an old California dish with a marvelous smell and a divine taste. Many of the other dishes had been prepared by Damo Vuletich, a cosmopolitan artist, chef, and old friend of Hattie's family. He looked like Picasso and was a great cook, but I had my reservations about his painting ability. Once after a wonderful dinner at his Carmel studio we were subjected to an endless review of his small sketches, painted in Europe the previous year on an extended trip he'd made with another artist friend. Out of gratitude for his fine cooking I wanted to say something nice about his art work, but I couldn't. The last two paintings of the

Le Depression days,

SCALES (in FISH WEIGHING TOWER)

Mrs. Gragg, at the head of the table, was dressed in a long red velvet gown. She had a shock of thick white hair and an imperious manner. She tapped on her wine glass with her table knife for attention.

"I'd like to propose a toast to one of our four honored guests," she said graciously. I noticed John Steinbeck, across the table, looking self-consciously at his plate, but for once he was mistaken.

"To Jean Ariss," Mrs. Gragg proposed, "probably the most beautiful and dangerous woman to come to Monterey since Lola Montez!"

There was a murmur of applause and a clinking of long stemmed goblets. Jean blushed a bright red and protested she was only a simple country girl and certainly not to be classed with that internationally famous Spanish beauty of the past century. I'd been doing some research on Lola Montez for a prospective mural, and to cover Jean's obvious embarrassment, I jumped in with some information about Lola. Contrary to popular belief, there is no proof that she had ever performed at California's First Theater in Monterey, back in the Gold Rush days. As nearly as I could discover, she'd gone straight from New York to the Mother Lode where all the men and action were, in those times. Actually, Monterey had become a ghost town. Even the soldiers at the Presidio had deserted to the mines.

Lola's legendary beauty had made her the mistress of the Emperor Frederick II of Bavaria. His lavish gifts to her had bankrupted the country and his councillors had finally run her out of town. She came to America and became the toast of New York.

It is a strange commentary on the times that, in the so-called anti-aristocratic United States, Lola was idolized as though she were an empress herself. American males lined up for blocks outside her New York hotel room, where she languished on a chaise lounge. They filed in reverently, kissed her hand, murmured a few compliments, and left. Some of them, like soldiers in wartime at a bordello, even went out and got in line for another go around. She was an indifferent actress,

group were not so bad, however, so I opened up on them and waxed lyrical in my praise, telling Damo he should try to paint that way all the time. Damo accepted my compliments rather taciturnly, I thought, and on the way home in the old Franklin, Gus Gay told me why. The last two paintings had been by his friend, and I hadn't given Damo a chance to explain that before I launched into my paeans of praise.

Damo wore a very tall chef's hat, which made him look very professional, while he helped out at Mrs. Gragg's banquet. The old pink plastered adobe walls must have seen many such stately dinners in the days of the dons. In the distant gloom above the table the great rafters slowly salted the expansive dinner table with a gentle rain of termite droppings. We thought it was a fine evening all around.

however. Her first play was harshly abused by the critics. Lola went to the editor's office of one of the big New York journals and worked him over with a horsewhip. Standard practice then, apparently, and easier than writing a letter of protest.

Lola left for Virginia City, where she became the first citizen of that old Nevada gold town. When she died, years later, it turned out she wasn't Spanish after all. Her real name was Liza Gilbert, she'd been born in Brooklyn, and had gone to Europe as a young dancer and invented herself.

When I'd finished, Mrs. Gragg asked Ed and John to say a few words about the Baja trip, which they did—very few. In the midst of this pleasant exchange over good food someone yelled "Fire!" Gus Gay, sitting just beyond Marcelle on my right, had laid his old briar pipe on the table, and a coal had fallen out and ignited the lace heirloom. Gus dumped his full glass of red wine over it, while Marcelle gave him hell under his breath for his social blundering. Mrs. Gragg, the perfect hostess, went right on talking as though nothing had happened.

I'd donated a woodblock cut to the Carmel *Cymbal* depicting Hitler and Mussolini dressed in Spanish matador costumes, marching into a bull ring, side by side, giving the fascist salute. It was quite popular, and soon after I was contacted by the *People's World,* a Communist daily paper published in San Francisco. They wanted to know if I'd do editorial cartoons for them for pay. I could have used the extra money but I turned them down. I figured they'd probably want me to join the Party, and I was leery of that. It wasn't illegal then, but Communists were such zealots they wouldn't let you alone to think for yourself. I felt their Marxist dogma was even more narrow and limiting than the Catholicism from which I'd escaped as a kid.

Leftist publications were always pestering Steinbeck for contributions too, but he avoided them. His strike novel had been sympathetic to the workers, but he didn't want to be identified with any doctrinaire party line, either.

About that time, when the violent lettuce strike was going on in nearby Salinas, the word was given to the WPA artists that they'd have to pick lettuce as strikebreakers, or lose their subsistence art jobs. To a man they refused, and nothing was done about it. The Roosevelt administration, in general, was labor oriented, so that particular pressure campaign must have been slipped through a back door, somehow, probably through the efforts of the local growers' associations. They did manage to get Salinas high school kids to pick their lettuce.

One pleasant day Ed drove Jean and me up to Los Gatos to see John and Carol in their new house.

John had described it as "a little shack in the mountains," but it was quite the opposite. It seemed very new and very grand to Jean and me. It was large and roomy, at least compared to our 10 x 20 cabin in Pacific Grove. As I remember, there was a sunny split-level living room with a big fireplace at the lower end. Carol was seated in front of the big used red-brick wall of the fireplace, arguing over an opened roll of house plans with the young contractor-carpenter. He wore a plaid shirt that was red, as was his face, as he dickered angrily with Carol over some of the finicky details of the job.

John, Ed, Jean, and I retired to the upper level where John showed us a small writing den opening off the far end of the dining area. John liked to write in confined spaces. Along the east side of the big living room there was an outside balcony with a western paddock-style balustrade. We stepped out on it and John pointed out the limits of his two-acre plot. The land dropped away to a wooded creek then rose to a hilly area to the north. John pointed to the neighboring ranch where an old man on a ladder was pruning his apple trees.

"See that old neighbor of mine?" he chuckled. "He's quite a Down-East character. Taciturn, to say the least. Wouldn't even say hello the first few times I ran into him. Finally I told him 'I'm John Steinbeck.' 'Hmp!' he says, 'Who's he?' Apparently never heard of me! Isn't that great? That's just why I moved out here."

Jean scowled and shaded her eyes. "He doesn't look so mean to me," she said brightly. "I bet he's a sweet old man and you just rubbed him the wrong way. I bet he'd talk to me."

"Nonsense," John said scornfully. "He'd cut you dead."

"I'll take that chance," Jean said devilishly. She popped down the back steps of the balcony and danced across the field towards the old man.

John, Ed, and I followed after her more slowly.

"She's crazy," John complained. "Pretty girls think they can get away with anything. You'll see. She'll meet her match, this time."

We watched up ahead as Jean scrambled over the rail fence and went to the foot of the ladder. She said something to the old man. He climbed down briskly, threw his arms around her, and kissed her.

"I'll be goddamned!" John exploded. "I can't believe it! What'd she say to him?"

"I said hello, Uncle Will," Jean grinned as we came up. "This is my father's cousin, Will Fitch. I thought it might be him when I saw him from a distance, but I couldn't be sure 'til I got over here. Isn't it a weird coincidence? I used to spend all my summers on this ranch when I was a kid. I had a feeling this area looked awfully familiar."

John still had one foot in both camps. He was more comfortable writing in his old Pacific Grove house, so if Carol and the contractor were working on any noisy finishing details in the new house, he drove back to the Pacific Grove place. He felt he did his best work there. He planned to maintain the family cottage on Eleventh Street always, and in fact came back there, off and on, almost to the end of his life.

John and Carol had relaxed their economy enough to buy a new car, a very conservative small black Chevy sedan. John wanted to get rid of his old car, a '23 Dodge roadster that had seen better days and was just sitting in the street, now that the new car was in the alley garage. He told me one morning he'd given the Dodge to Francis Whitaker, the thorny Carmel blacksmith, who made the fireplace cone that John had installed in his living room. I drove the old Dodge over the hill for John. Afterwards we went to the Lab, where everyone was arguing about politics, mostly on the pros and cons of the Spanish Civil War.

The heated argument was cut short by sudden shrieking blasts from a dozen surrounding cannery whistles. It was noon time already. Suzy Herman, the willowy artists' model, changed the subject.

"I'm hungry. Let's go the King Cafe for lunch."

Some of us didn't have enough to make the 26¢, so we were rearranging our pennies for those who were short. Suddenly John stood up with an angry oath.

"You guys can waste your money on restaurant food if you want to," he said irritably. "Not me! I'm going home and open up a can of Monterey sardines!" He stormed out of the room and down the steps.

The rest of us looked at each other in surprise. "What brought that on?" someone asked.

"His conscience must be hurting him," I said. "I was over to his house this morning and he was hunting through his rolltop desk for the owner's certificate for his old car. On top of his mail was a check from his publisher for $5,000. He showed it to me and said 'Look at all this dough! What the hell am I supposed do with it?' And in great contempt he flips it back on the mail pile. I was gonna say, 'Listen, if it's that much trouble, just give it to me. Jean and I could live at our standard for the next ten years on it, or more, without any problems.' But I didn't say it. I knew he was just showing off. And besides, it wasn't really his money. Carol has that five grand already earmarked for their new house in Los Gatos. Or maybe their rainy day bank account."

I went back to work on my WPA mural. I was making a full-sized cartoon on brown wrapping paper. I needed a working wall about eighteen feet wide and ten feet high. My cabin was too small and even the Lab basement was too crowded. Remo had rented a big old house on Fourth Street where he was doing a WPA statue of Father Serra in the front yard. He said I was welcome to use his living room for a work space.

Jean posed for the main figure of California, a seated Indian girl of massive proportions. Standing, the figure would have been almost ten feet tall. Remo chopped away at the statue and occasionally posed for me as an early California don. It was a pleasant and creative interlude.

Remo's house had one of the shortest claw-foot tubs I'd ever seen, but plenty of automatic hot water. When she wasn't typing away at her short stories, or posing for the mural, Jean spent most of the time reading in the tub, her long legs folded up like a grasshopper's.

By the time I finished my big full-scale colored chalk cartoon, the WPA office had found me a better studio in the Old Pacific Building. It was a large Mexican adobe in downtown Monterey, owned by the Jacks' sisters. I moved in all my painting gear and worked away at at the big egg tempera, mixing some of the colors I'd brought from the Lab with egg yolks and sun-thickened linseed stand oil. It was a medium originated in the Egyptian tomb paintings, but I was following the later Renaissance Italian formula of Cenino. I'd been greatly influenced by the work of Diego Rivera in art school, and I'd made a block cut portrait of him for the *Occident.* Rivera said it was the best portrait that had been done of him to date, which was quite a feather in a young art student's cap.

Rivera's painting technique consisted of short, narrow brush strokes about two inches long. I must have made several hundred thousand of these many-colored brush strokes by the time I finished the mural, working long hours in the excitement of trying to complete it. When it was all done, I found I had a bad case of double vision. I stumbled to a nearby optometrist who sold me a fine pair of new glasses that made me see single again. I went to bed and slept for two days. When I woke up my vision was back to normal, but when I put on my new glasses I saw double!

The Lab burned to the ground that autumn.

Jean and I had gone up to my folks' place in Berkeley, one hundred miles north of Monterey, for an annual Thanksgiving family feast. We heard the news on the radio:

> All of the northwest end of Cannery Row is in flames. Nothing will be left standing.

We went out into the night street and saw the tinged sky from Berkeley.

When we got back to Cannery Row the following evening, it looked like it had been blitzed. Smoking hills

BOX NAILING MACHINE

Salinas Lettuce Strike Bruce Ariss 1936

of charred timbers writhed amongst smelly mountains of burned sardine cans in every direction. Occasionally, an overheated can in one of the steaming mounds would explode like a small bomb and pop ten or fifteen feet up into the air. The noble fire laddies had managed to save Flora Wood's valued bordello, across the street from Ed's, but nothing else on the water side. Wing Chong's little grocery, and La Ida, the next largest whorehouse on the Row, also escaped. We found Ed forlornly inspecting the flattened rubble that had once been the Lab. Everything was gone, his library, his scientific papers, his fine record collection, all the stored bottles of specimens and, of course, all my beautiful jars of colors. The only thing that survived was a fireproof safe that had stood beside the rolltop desk in the upstairs entry office. It was sitting in the ashes on the ground. Ed opened it and found some smelly cheese he stored there the day before the fire.

Actually, Ed seemed quite philosophic about it. He'd barely escaped with his life. The fire had burst out from an enormous electrical short in the cannery adjoining the Lab. In the middle of the night, the flames had shot right through the wall above the bed where he was sleeping. He only had time to grab his pants and flee, barefooted and barechested, down the steps.

Everyone did what they could for Ed. Clothes, books, and records were collected for him. John swung a loan for rebuilding. Remo drew the plans and the carpenters tried to restore the Lab, as much as possible, just as it had been before the fire. Life went on.

With the Lab gone, we had to find other places for the Lab Group to gather—at John's Eleventh Street cottage when he was in town, at Remo's studio on Fourth, or in our little cabin on Ninth.

The WPA had an even bigger mural for me to do, so I decided I had to start my new studio on Huckleberry Hill. Besides, Jean was expecting our first baby and we had to have more room to raise a family. I scoured the countryside in my little Ford truck, picking up second-hand lumber. It was before radar was invented and I salvaged many ships' timbers from wrecks along the coast. It was impossibly hard work, but I had more energy than brains or money. John enjoyed watching my progress and came up often, shaking his head in amazement at my frantic efforts. He said I was a big overgrown beaver.

"Where'd you get all this mess of lumber and timbers?" he demanded one day.

I laughed and told him about my floating Fort Ticonderoga. Romey Jacks had planned to build another luxury hotel. He started out with a great flourish, built huge forms on Carmel Hill, and poured the foundations. The '29 Market Crash stopped everything in its tracks. They didn't even strip the form lumber off the concrete, just walked off and left everything.

In the spring of 1937, when I was working on the walls of my studio, I heard that old Jock McCullogh was stripping the form lumber from the Romey Jacks hotel, and it was all for sale. I fired up my little old Ford flatrack and trundled over to the site.

I asked "old man" McCullogh, "How much for a truckload of lumber?"

"In that little puddle jumper?" Old Mac was a sarcastic one-eyed skinflint, and he always drove a hard bargain. He sniffed contemptuously at my Ford and rasped, "All the lumber you can get on that thing, you can have for ten bucks." He snatched my ten spot and drove off in his long car.

I winked at the men working on the forms, most of whom I knew. Many were hard-up WPA workers and artists trying to earn a few extra bucks in their spare time by working *sub rosa* for the miserly old salvageman. They understood my wink, chuckled, and hopped to it. We laid some ten foot timbers across the rack and piled huge twenty-four foot timbers lengthwise, extending a good five feet beyond the front and back of the truck. We stacked it up ten feet high. There must have been ten thousand board feet loaded on to that poor shuddering little vehicle. It's a wonder all the tires didn't explode at once.

I sneaked the truck past the police station to the foot of Huckleberry Hill. Then I had to back the truck up for two miles uphill, standing on the bonnet, peering over the top of the load, and steering through the open windshield with my foot.

"It looks just like Fort Ticonderoga," someone shouted. John and I had a good laugh over the incident.

John, though he was now living permanently in Los Gatos, came back often to the Lab, his house in the Grove, or to watch my progress on the Hill. He was also making frequent trips to New York and Hollywood. Money wasn't as tight as it used to be. John was even planning a trip to Europe in the near future with Carol, by freighter.

Of Mice and Men, in spite of my dire prediction in Baja about its not selling, was apparently making nothing but money. John was also talking about going East to work with George Kaufman, the New York director, on a stage production of *Mice and Men*.

We moved into the unfinished studio when the baby was only a few weeks old. The only problem we had with him as he grew was toilet training. We'd sit him on the pot in the yard, under the pine trees in the sunshine, but he'd just sit there, scream, cry, and shake his fists. John came up and watched in disgust.

"What the hell you trying to do? Make a sissy out of that kid? He doesn't want to pee sitting down. He wants to stand up like a man! Hell, you haven't even cut off those long blond baby curls of his yet. Here, let me show you."

John grabbed our little boy by the waist and stood him on his feet. They strode off to our front gate. With their backs to us, and their legs wide apart, they both wet down the bushes satisfactorily. They came back with a look of triumph on their faces.

"What did I tell you?" John grinned. "There was nothing to it!"

I hesitate to recount the incident, not from any sense of violating propriety, but rather because of a fear I have that one of the many Steinbeck commemorative societies, upon reading this, might strike a bronze plaque and nail it lowdown on my gatepost, rather like the signs on the New England inns that noted that George Washington slept there.

Ridiculous? Well, not really. It wasn't too long ago

that I went to a Salinas memorial celebration where a hundred high school kids had been formed into two glee clubs to sing John's praises. The boys' group wore white sweaters with the phrase "John Steinbeck is My Friend" printed across their chests. The girls' sweaters had a red heart cut-out that read "I Love John Steinbeck." All this in a town where, a few years previously, John had felt that their parents and grandparents had hated him so much he feared they might actually try to lynch him. As I listened incredulously to the young singers, I wondered what John would have done if he were alive and sitting beside me. I could only imagine him putting his handkerchief over his mouth and crashing for the nearest men's room.

But back on Huckleberry Hill, in those early days, I was only amused and somewhat surprised by John's brusque but expert handling of a child-training situation that had baffled Jean and me for weeks.

In spite of John's unexpected expertise with children, Dr. Evelyn Ott came to me with a request.

"I've watched you with your own boy, and with Ed Junior," she said gravely. "You have a comfortable way with children. My six-year-old, little Peter, worries me a great deal. I've been divorced so long he doesn't remember his father. He has no male image in his life. I was wondering if I could pay you to give him boxing lessons, and teach him to ride a bicycle, and so on? It would be only on Saturday mornings. He's started school, but he's very unhappy. I'd be willing to pay you very well for your time."

"That wouldn't be necessary," I said. "I'd be glad to help out." But Dr. Ott insisted, and since psychiatrists seemed to be among the lucky few who had no worries about money during the Depression, I finally accepted payment.

A psychoanalyst's fee was $25 an hour—a fantastic amount of money in those days. Like many doctors, and others to whom money came easily, Evelyn felt a little guilty about it. She preferred not to handle her funds herself. She turned her finances over to a business manager who'd put her earnings into stocks and bonds. She told me she'd recently discovered that a substantial part of her investments were in a Snelling gold dredge venture. She heard I'd worked in the Sierra gold mines. Did I know what Snelling was?

"Hell, yes," I told her. "That's right next to where I was working at La Grange. Do you own stock in that outfit? Those dredges are huge. Over two hundred feet long and almost a hundred feet wide, they're like big floating warehouses with teeth. It used to make me sick what those big monsters did to the landscape. I'd drive past there every day on the way to the big open placer mine where I worked. One day there'd be a marvelous Corot pastoral scene, with black and white cattle grazing along the river banks under the tall trees. The next day everything was gone. Overnight that enormous dredger had chewed up the countryside like a giant locust. All that was left were piles of naked boulders stacked in the mud. The trees, the river banks, everything—all gone. Even the cows had disappeared, though I don't suppose the dredge had ground them up into hamburger. It was a criminal devastation. A million year old landscape wiped out in one day. Of course, we were placer mining, too, but it was up on the barren foothills, so it wasn't such an obvious act of vandalism, but it was awful what those damned dredges did to the scenery."

The following week, Dr. Ott drove the one hundred miles over to Snelling to see for herself. When she returned she was even more outraged and indignant than I'd been. Without a word of explanation to her broker she ordered him to immediately unload all her dredger stock. I wondered, at the time, if Evelyn's precipitous selling might not have had a disastrous effect on the fragile local stock market, but if it had, I didn't hear anything about it.

Teaching little Peter to box was something else again. The boy was so limp and lackadaisical that it was pitiful. He had about as much vitality as a wet potato chip. He was extremely small for his age and when he put on my big yellow horsehide sparring gloves they reached almost to his armpits. He couldn't seem to get the idea of punching. He'd just push gently with a sweet, apologetic smile. I think he was the only kid I ever failed to teach to box.

I did everything I could. I'd poke him gently in the face. I'd tousle his blond cornsilk hair over his baby blue eyes, trying to arouse in him some sense of combativeness. No luck. No matter what I did to antagonize him, he just smiled and looked at me adoringly. I suppose he just liked the attention, even if he didn't know why I was waving at him and pushing him around. Or maybe he was a natural born pacifist? I stuck out my jaw and yelled "Hit me! Hit me!," but he'd just pat my face shyly. I was sure my two-year old son would have decked him with one punch.

I worked patiently for months. Every Saturday we'd go around, but it didn't do any good. I finally gave up and just went through the motions. The one positive thing I was able to do for him was to teach him to ride his two-wheeled bike. It had been stuck in the garage since the previous Christmas. He'd shown no interest in it. I perched him firmly on the bicycle's seat and pushed him all around Carmel. About the second time around town I was getting bushed. Fortunately, just before we reached his house, it somehow occurred to him there might be a purpose to all this. He started to pump on the pedals and I let go. He wobbled up his driveway on his own power, with a look of wonder on his small, pinched face. There were accompanying screams of delight from his mother, who just at the moment happened out on the porch.

I kept on trying to teach little Peter to be a fighter. It was hopeless. It began to be a chore and I was trying to think of some way to end the program gracefully, even though I'd come to rely on the money. One morning I came half an hour late for the lesson. Peter was not sitting limply on the porch, where he usually waited for me. I strolled around toward the back of the house, looking for him.

Suddenly there was a blood-curdling scream. Little Peter exploded down out of a tree onto my shoulders and began pummeling me over the head with a stick. I untangled him and lowered him to the ground. With wild Indian warwhoops he leaped on his bike and pedaled off down the street. Evelyn came out on the porch, laughing and wiping her eyes.

Steinbeck + new car? Holman's Parking Lot (About 1940?) *A big '39 Lincoln?

The Great sans-Culotte!

"What the hell's going on around here?" I asked in astonishment.

"It's so funny! Evelyn was chuckling helplessly. "I'm a medical doctor, too, you know, so last night I gave him a male hormone shot, to see if I couldn't arouse some interest in the boxing lessons. He was up at dawn this morning.. He used his scout knife to form that club he cut from a tree branch. Then he climbed up in the tree and waited all morning so he could ambush you. Isn't this all strange and ridiculous?"

Dr. Ott and I had a satisfying moment of communion in our laughter. Peter pedaled slowly back toward us, and that day, for the first time, the boxing lessons went fairly well.

It wasn't until quite a few years later, after the war, that I ran into Evelyn Ott again, in, of all places, the Carmel Women's Club. The speaker at the large meeting was a former acquaintance of mine who had become a well-known world traveler and lecturer. I'd thought I might slip in and do a story about him for my magazine. The lecture had already started. I took an empty seat near the back of the room which was crowded with elderly well-dressed ladies. The woman in the seat next to me turned large eyes of recognition on me.

CUTTING CHAINS

It was Evelyn Ott, and I was surprised how old and frail she looked. I'd thought she was about Steinbeck's age, but she now looked ten years older than he. She'd always been stylishly thin, but it had been more than a half dozen years since I'd seen her last, and now she looked almost skeletal, even ethereal. She'd changed so drastically, in such a short time really, that it crossed my mind that she might be suffering from some sort of life-threatening illness. Since she seemed as warm and outgoing as ever, I stopped myself from asking her any personal questions about her health.

The women's club lecturer was a mawkish guy who was buttering up all the old ladies in a disgusting exhibition of "momism." Evelyn and I looked at each other with expressions of distaste. In the midst of his ingratiating bath of syrup the lecturer recognized me and stopped short.

"Ah, I see we have one intrepid male in the audience," he said, clearing his throat. "I recognize him, and welcome him. He's an old friend of mine and a reporter, so I'd better settle down and get a little more serious with this lecture."

He did so, and the rest of his talk was quite presentable. I'd changed my mind about doing a story on him, however, and ducked out with Evelyn as soon as the lecture was over.

"What in the name of heaven were you doing at a lecture like that?" she demanded. I told her, and then asked her the same question.

"I really don't know," she replied reflectively. "I suppose it's because I'm a member."

We went to a sweet shop and lingered over cups of coffee, talking about old times. Ed was dead and John had gone on to New York and apparently more exalted things. He'd rarely returned to the Peninsula in the last few years, after Ed was gone.

I told her about the last time I saw him. I'd parked my old Dodge touring car in Holman's parking lot and was just coming out of their basement hardware store. Parked next to my old car was the most extravagant and vulgar-looking big car I'd ever seen. It was a huge open touring car, a half mile long, and covered with so much chrome-plated extras I couldn't tell what make it was. A Packard, a Lincoln, or a Cadillac? I walked around it in amazement, looking at all the shiny exhaust pipes, fender-welled spare tires, and noticing there was even a complete chrome-barred windshield for the back seat. Underneath all this I recognized a silvery whippet ornament on the radiator cap. Ah! It must be one of those new custom-built Lincoln Continentals? I shook my head, trying to recall Thorstein Veblen's phrases about Conspicuous Waste and The Theory of the Leisure Class.

I must have had a look of scornful disbelief and disgust on my face. I heard someone clearing his throat in embarrassment. I stood up and saw it was John Steinbeck standing beside me. This was his car! That great Sans Culotte, who swore never to let success change his life-style! I couldn't believe my eyes. We shook hands perfunctorily. I was still working on my studio and dressed in my carpenter's overalls. John was in a yachting costume: scrambled egg-covered officer's cap, blue-striped pullover sweater, starchy white ducks, and sneakers. Since I saw him last he must have put on twenty or thirty pounds, mostly around the middle, and his face was flushed a royal purple. From over-indulgence, I thought, plus, perhaps, the embarrassment of seeing my scornful reaction to his ornate automobile. He wore an expensive pair of wraparound sunglasses with polished brass frames that made him look like a highway motorcycle cop. I had a hard time seeing his eyes behind the dark lenses, but they certainly weren't looking directly at me.

I'd heard from friends who saw John in the East that he'd become quite a *boulevardier*, an habitué of Club 21, even sporting a Sandeman-type cape and hat with a new goatee, and, someone said, he even wore a monocle—though I couldn't believe that one. Still, one of the few times his new wife Gwyn (she changed her name from plain Gwen) showed up at the Lab, she stared down her nose at everyone through a long handled jeweled lorgnette.

We exchanged a few words. John said he'd been working hard in New York on a new book, but had decided to drive out to the Coast with his new wife in his new car. He said he was sorry, he'd only be in town a few days, and was late for a doctor's appointment, good-bye, see you around. He drove off hastily with a roar of twin silvered exhaust pipes. I stared after him, trying to recall those immortal lines of his in *The Grapes of Wrath* where he'd so bitterly described the wealthy limousines on Highway 66 speeding past the old dust bowl jalopies.

Evelyn seemed somewhat distressed by my story, and I suddenly remembered she'd always been one of John's most loyal boosters around the Lab. I decided to change the subject by asking about her son, Peter. She looked even more distressed.

"You haven't heard? He's dead."

"What? God, no, I hadn't heard. I'm sorry! What happened?"

She told me the painful story, in her slow, gently modulated voice. Peter had managed to get through the public schools and was finishing high school in Carmel. He'd never been happy, and always had been a loner. The one thing he owed to me, she said, was my teaching him to ride his bicycle. He'd made solitary bike trips on weekends for years. Then he developed diabetes and had been forced to take daily insulin shots, restrict his diet, and so on. He was terribly depressed about it. One day, he simply disappeared.

They had all points bulletins out on him for weeks. Two school kids, hiking along the Carmel River, discovered his body. He'd crawled deep into the brush, pulling his bike in after him. The ground around him was covered with empty forbidden candy wrappers. He'd gone into insulin shock and quietly died.

I felt terrible about Peter and said what I could, trying to console her. She started to laugh and cry at the same time, recalling little Peter astride my shoulders and beating on me with his home-made shillelagh and giving the Tarzan yell.

We parted company reluctantly, saying we should get

together, but that was the last time I saw her. I heard that her health had rapidly deteriorated. She retired from her practice and died shortly thereafter.

She was a lovely, sensitive, and quite tragic lady. I'm sure that, except for Ed, she had more influence on John's philosophy and writing than anyone else in his lifetime.

But to get back to John's way with children, prior to the potty training incident, I had my doubts about John and babies. Months earlier, when little Bruce was just born, John had leaned over his bassinette and looked at him fiercely.

"Little babies give me the willies," he announced violently. "They're so damn soft and mushy-looking! No bones in them. The only thing they're good for is to pick them up by the hind legs and smack their brains out against a wall!"

He said this with such harsh conviction that I instinctively stepped between he and the bassinette.

"What the hell are you talking about?" I demanded, wondering if he possibly could be as serious as he sounded. He just shrugged and walked off. A funny guy! I had to admit I didn't understand him half the time. Yet later, in his second marriage, he'd apparently been a good father to his own two sons, though I've been told they don't remember him too fondly. Once, when the boys were about fourteen and fifteen, they asked if they could visit the Lab while on a vacation here.

Ed was dead, and a bunch of us had bought the Lab to preserve it as a club and sort of literary monument. I was going out of town that day, but I gave the keys to Jean to take the boys , Thom and John, through. She said the oldest boy, Thom, had expressed his annoyance that he'd not been the one named after his famous father.

Cannery Row changed greatly after the war. As Ed had predicted, the mass canning and over-fishing during the wartime had broken up the great schools and interrupted the sardines' reproduction cycle. The catches dwindled to almost nothing. Of course, the canners and the fishermen claimed it wasn't their fault. Mostly they blamed the Japanese. Their submarines had frightened away the sardines. Or, the Japanese current had shifted and driven the fish to another part of the Pacific. In any case, the canneries soon closed for lack of fish. The Row became a graveyard of rusting machinery. The gloomy profile of the big buildings against the sky was broken here and there by toothless gaps where, it was hinted, some of the disgruntled canners had torched their own establishments in an attempt to collect some insurance money out of the calamity.

The first book of John's to be published after the War was *Cannery Row*, a more or less comic description of the Row in its earlier sardine-filled days. Before he sent it to his publishers, John showed the typed manuscript to Ed. His friend shrugged it off indulgently, even though he realized that the main character in the book, "Doc," was so obviously supposed to be himself that it would, as he told us, "probably change my life forever." It certainly did. He was bothered by curious tourists almost every day thereafter, while trying to get his work done downstairs in the Lab, which was usually open to the street.

The rest of the Lab Group, who read the book after it was published, were not as indulgent as Ed had been. We thought it was a patronizing misrepresentation, projecting on Ed the materialistic and sensual qualities that were more John's than Ed's. The book was to bring hordes of tourists to Monterey, looking for John's fictional Row. These tourists shored up the sag in the local economy caused by the disappearance of the sardines.

Most of our friends, unlike the sardines, made it back to the area after the war. Many started to build studios on Huckleberry Hill. When the land ran out, an overflow colony sprang up in the nearby woods of Del Monte Park, which I facetiously re-christened Raspberry Flat.

There was a fine new vigor in the air. Trees going down, houses going up. It was like an early pioneer community of the Old West. We even held an old-fashioned house-building bee. In a wild eight hours a dozen of us put up a complete studio home of donated

HAPPY NEW YEAR
ATOMIC YEAR THREE
...But they did eat of the fruit of the Tree of Knowledge...

My Dantesque greeting card in 1947 — (After the engraving style of Gustave Doré)

materials, as a surprise for a young Mexican artist friend and his homeless family. They reciprocated by starting an excellent Mexican restaurant in their front room and refusing payment from their friends who built it.

John was spending most of his time in New York or Mexico after the war. The artists' and writers' parties started up again at Ed's Lab, at the new little Pat Wall modern art gallery down by Fisherman's Wharf, and at the various studios on the Hill.

A big disruption at one party happened over Suzy Herman, who Steinbeck was to describe later in his Cannery Row books. John denied this, of course. Any resemblance between fictional and real-life persons, etc. We'd given John such a bad time about defaming Ed in the book that he protested defensively that his prostitute, Suzy, was not our model Suzy. "I just liked the name— that's all."

Suzy had been separated from her very jealous husband, Hank, and he appeared at the party, put a gun (with blanks) to her forehead, and fired. Suzy went over backwards. We drove her to the Lab, still half hysterical, and Ed gave her first aid for the powder burn above her eyes.

She slept with Ed that night, but in the morning, over coffee, she was indignant and very angry with Ed.

"He held me all night. Comforted me like a baby. But he didn't even try to make love to me! Am I that damned unattractive?"

Another memorable party was the one at Peggy and Toby Streets' housewarming on Carmel Point. A hard headed Swedish writer, who made his living as an ice man, got terribly drunk and obnoxious and began beating up on the women and smaller men in at the party. They sent me in as reinforcement.

I caught him with my first outraged punch on the side of his head. He folded his wings and flew, three feet off the floor, clear across the living room. When he hit the far wall everyone thought there was an earthquake. He picked himself up and went home very quietly.

The biggest and wildest party of all was the famous one that wrecked the Lab and figured in John's books about Cannery Row. This particular party was a gathering that started out quietly as a pleasant discussion group. Jean's brother Bryant who studied with Einstein at Cal Tech had

fish oil Centrifigal Separators

flown up from Southern California to visit us. He and Ed got along well and were always deep in scientific talk. Gustaf Lannestook, the Swedish translator, brought his houseguests, a Hollywood screenwriter and his wife. The writer's name was Bruce Lockheed. To make things more complicated, Bruce's wife was named Jean.

She was eight months pregnant with their first child, and the two Jeans went off immediately into a neutral corner to talk baby-care problems. Bruce was a talented story teller, and full of exciting yarns about international intrigue. He was supposed to have been the guy that Ian Fleming used as a model for those 007 superspy novels. There were several other unusually interesting persons who were in and out of the party, so it was certainly not the roomful of Doc's drunken Cannery Row bums that Steinbeck was to make of it some years later. John, himself, was away in Europe, or some other far place. He only heard reports of the fracas, second-hand from Ed, weeks afterward.

About eight o'clock, when we were getting hungry, most of us drove off in three cars to Mr. Chan's little Shanghai Low restaurant. It was a small family-style place, but quite a step above the cheaper King Cafe. Ed stopped on the way at the Knotty Pine Inn to buy a big bottle of rum to spike the tea.

We drove back to the Lab and Ed stopped to buy another bottle of rum. The discussions at Ed's place began to grow somewhat noisier. We ran out of rum once again. Lockheed asked his wife for the keys to their car, so he could drive back to the Knotty Pine Inn for another bottle. He was in no condition to drive, and his wife flatly told him so. She shook her head firmly, and dropped the keys down inside the neckline of her blouse.

Bruce turned suddenly into a violently mean drunk. He tore open her shirt and tried to find the keys inside her brassiere while she fought him off. When he couldn't locate the keys, he was so frustrated he slugged her in the jaw. She went down, hitting her head on Ed's big iron Franklin stove, which sat in the corner by the door into the kitchen. Bruce leaned over her drunkenly, still trying to get at the keys.

My Jean, as always the protective and militant feminist, jumped into the struggle to try to fend off the snarling husband. He swung, hitting her on the jaw, too, and my Jean went down on the floor beside the other Jean. They were both unconscious.

Bruce was shaking his wife roughly, still trying to get her to relinquish the car keys. Everything had happened so suddenly that the others just stood around frozen, with their mouths open. My Jean came to, scrambled to her feet, and once again jumped between the husband battering away at his pregnant wife. Jean was hell bent on protecting the next generation!

Bruce slugged her again and this time my Jean went down, hitting her head on the Franklin stove, too, to lie there unconscious. It was getting so repetitious. I stood up, feeling a powerful surge of ancestral Irish rage.

"Listen, Lockheed," I yelled. "Maybe you can knock my wife down once, but Goddamn it, you can't do it twice."

I stepped toward him. He was obviously out of control and I hoped to get this thing over as quickly as possible. I hit him in the face with a long straight left jab. I wanted to turn his jaw up for the short right hook I hoped would put him out of his misery for a good five minutes or so. I never threw that second punch. To my amazement his nose exploded like an over-ripe tomato thrown against a concrete wall. He told us later that he'd been tortured in a Russian prison camp and his whole face subsequently had to be rebuilt by plastic surgery. His wife was also to tell us that he was a former alcoholic, who'd been dried out for seven years before the night of this impossible party.

His nose spouted blood like a crimson fountain. He began leaping around the room, imitating a Mexican jumping bean, holding both hands over his gory face, and bellowing with rage and pain. You could hear him roaring curses from one end of Cannery Row to the other. He began throwing wild punches at me through the spray of bloody vapor coming from his nose. He was like a harpooned and enraged Moby Dick, bent on blind vengeance.

Lockheed's bellowing bull-like rushes were creating havoc in the Lab. He was knocking over tables, chairs, lamps, and everything else that was loose in the room. A large, free-standing bookcase of Ed's precious and newly-collected library went over with a horrendous crash. Volumes went flying in every direction. People were screaming, "Bruce! Bruce!" or "Stop! Stop!" or "Hit him! Hit him again!" I didn't know which of the two Bruces they were imploring to stop or go in this crazy fight.

Lockheed's legs finally buckled, and he slumped to his knees with his face in his hands, though I still hadn't hit him a second time. He stopped roaring and began groaning instead. The blood was still streaming in rivers between his fingers. His wife thought we'd better get him to the hospital before he bled to death. Suzy had gone into Ed's kitchen to try to find a bowl to catch the gore, but couldn't locate one. She came back with a gallon fruit can that was half full of sugar, instead. They held up Bruce's lolling ahead and let the cascade of red blood fall into the white sugar. Finally his wife managed to organize a group of us to load him into their automobile for the hospital trip. She was so upset I feared she might have the baby at any minute, just to add to the absolute chaos of the evening.

My Jean was still dizzy from a knot on the back of her head. I decided to drive her home to bed. Ed was nowhere around to be seen. The next day he told us that his ulcer had begun to bother him at the party—from too much rum, combined with the rich chinese food—so he stepped out to walk on a nearby beach in the moonlight until he felt better. He said he left a very pleasant party of good people in serious conversation, with a classical fugue playing gently in the background on the phonograph.

When he returned it was a different scene entirely. Everyone was gone, the door was banging open in the wind, and his Lab was a catastrophe. It looked like a slaughterhouse. Every light that wasn't smashed was burning, and, of course, there was that grisly and inexplicable gallon tin of blood and sugar at the center of it all.

Ed admitted he had indulged in too much rum, but his head was beginning to clear. He was absolutely baffled. He said he suddenly recalled the old story of how Lord Nelson, his legs blown off in his final shipboard battle, was stood on his bloody stumps in a half barrel of sand by his weeping sailors. Ed said he had this crazy vision of a miniature Admiral Nelson, twelve inches high, bleeding to death in his sugar pot.

This riotous evening inspired the Wild Party sequence about the wrecking of Doc's Lab in Steinbeck's *Cannery Row*.

What none of us knew until long afterward was that Bruce Lockheed was an imposter. The real British Agent was named Bruce Lockhart, Lord Hamilton. The Bruce who came to Monterey had passed himself off in the film capital as the member of the British Foreign Office who had written the 007 autobiographical best-seller. His phony British accent and monocle had fooled the film people just as much as he fooled Gustaf Lannestock, Ed, and all the rest of us at the Lab in Monterey.

There was a general impression in town, no doubt inspired by John's salty books on Cannery Row, that Ed had always surrounded himself with bums, idiots, and other drifters. This was obviously untrue. In fact, we were amazed once to discover that our little group contained—more or less accidentally—five "termites." This was a nickname for members of Stanford University's Rockefeller-Terman study of the one thousand highest "genius IQs" tested among all the California school kids. The study had begun in the early twenties and carried on throughout the entire adult lives of the one thousand "guinea pig" geniuses.

John's brother-in-law, Bill Dekker, had been one. Ed's Toni Siexas Jackson was another. Remo's wife, Virginia was a third, and I was the fourth. Obviously Ed and John were outstanding "brains" themselves, but they'd been too old when the tests were made, and besides Ed had been raised in Illinois, not California. Jean was too young at the time of the testing, or she certainly would have rated as a top Termite. There were others in our group who were obviously bright enough—Ritchie, for example—but who'd been missed by the Terman dragnet, for one reason or another. One of the most quietly intellectual young men in the Lab Group was Milt Heifitz, a cousin of the famous violinist, a medical doctor doing his army stint at Fort Ord. He was later to become famous as one of the nation's leading brain surgeons. Another young army medic who frequented the Lab was Rick Skahen. I heard later that he was also a Termite, though he was so wildly extraverted that nobody suspected it. One of the most brilliant minds of our Cannery Row bunch was a young Iowa law student, Al Matthews, who later was to become a famous defense attorney and public defender in the Los Angeles area. Still another very bright guy, who dropped in frequently from San Francisco, was Hillary Belloc, the son of the famous British Apologist.

Ed felt it was statistically extraordinary that so many of the Terman Test Group should show up under his battered roof on Cannery Row, in such a small sidewater town as Monterey. Ed worked for a long time on an essay entitled "A Study of Genius," which I've never tried to read, possibly for fear I might not be able to understand it. Ed often lost me in his theoretical flights, particularly those he put down on paper.

CUTTING CHAINS

In the late 30s, quite some time after the Steinbecks came back from Europe, John made another quick trip to New York and back. He'd gone to confer with his publishers about some urgent problem or other with his forthcoming novel, *The Grapes of Wrath*. John was certain this new book would prove to be his definitive work, and didn't want anything to go wrong.

Some weeks later, when John got back to my studio, he was bursting with laughter. He told me a long, funny story about the trip, which, he said, had been completely unnecessary. He chuckled that it had all been a "tempest in a piss pot." It seems he received a frantic message from his publishers while he was in Los Gatos. They implied a very serious question had come up, but they couldn't tell him what it was over the telephone. Was it possible for him to fly back there immediately?

It wasn't really possible, in fact, it was damned inconvenient, to say the least, John told them. He felt they kept him criss-crossing the country when he only wanted to stay home and write. But he went anyway, because they'd sounded so somber and mysterious about it. Was there some sort of impending doom in the publishing business? Something he didn't know about? He'd always been punchy because two of his former publishers had collapsed under him in his early days. He'd put so much time and energy into this big new book, that he hated to think that anything could go wrong at this late date. What in hell could it be?

With a sense of foreboding, he said, he'd gone straight to his publishers' offices, without first checking into his hotel. The editor who'd contacted him turned out to be an elderly and very proper-looking Bostonian who reminded him of Marquand's *Late George Apley*. The man hemmed and hawed all around the subject. John couldn't figure out what was going on.

"For God's sake," John finally broke in. "Just tell me what's gone wrong!"

"Very well, then. Here's the problem." The Late George Apley seemed to be blushing furiously. "It's the word."

"The word? What word?"

"The one on page seventy-five. I'm sure you know the one I mean."

"I *don't* know. I can't remember the page numbers of my manuscripts! What word are you talking about?"

The editor wouldn't say it. John suddenly realized what was going on. The word was "fuck"—a word that was rarely printed in over-the-counter books in the late 1930s. The editor was so strait-laced he couldn't even say the word aloud! John realized this poor puritanical old bastard was going to try to convince him to eliminate the word from his book. John said he began laughing inwardly. He could have fun with this. Instantly he decided he'd never consent to his precious manuscript being bowdlerized by such a prissy old codger. He proceeded to needle the embarrassed editor mercilessly.

But before the Aquarium came and the S.P. tracks went... the old Boatworks on China Point was still in operation.

"Now sir," John said. "If you'll just come right out and say what this word is—right out loud—maybe we can make some sort of compromise. Now! What did you say that word was?"

John said it was impossible to get the old editor to say it. The poor guy finally searched through John's manuscript until he located the word. He pointed to it with his index finger.

"There," he whispered. "That's it."

"Oh, *that* one," John said so loudly he could be heard six offices away. "Oh! You mean FUCK! Hell, I couldn't possibly change *that* word! Fuck is the one indestructible word there is, nowadays. No way you can change it, or eliminate it, or improve on it. Fuck is the prime word, if not the primary activity of modern man. The English language has no single satisfactory substitute for it. It may be one of the earliest words in man's archaic vocabulary, probably just after mama and dada. It's certainly the most flexible. Fuck can be used as a noun, a verb, an adjective, as whatever part of speech you want it to be. Without the word fuck, one half of the working men in America would be unable to communicate with the other half. Industry would grind to a fucking standstill!"

John laughed uncontrollably at the memory of the interview. He said that the conservative old guy twitched six inches up off his chair every time John said the word. It made him feel like a devilish little kid again, pulling the legs off a helpless bug, leg by leg.

"Did they make you delete the word?" I asked.

"Hell, no! I wouldn't stand for that! It's staying in."

"Good for you! What's this new book about? Is it the one on the Dustbowl Okies?"

"Yeah, that's right. And it's as down-to-earth as I can make it. Good, basic stuff. I didn't let them pull my teeth on anything!"

John was elated by his triumph over those he felt were trying to curb his freedom of expression, but later John was to admit he actually had to make a number of changes and concessions in his manuscript. He stood firm on *The Word* however, and more importantly, on making any changes in the controversial and shocking finale where the young Okie woman who lost her baby gives her breast to the old man dying of malnutrition.

John went on to give me a short dissertation on the status of current censorship. "After all," he pointed out. "It's been a good five years since Judge Woolsey's *Ulysses* decision in the Supreme Court. We don't have to smuggle in Joyce or Frank Harris or Henry Miller anymore, in brown paper jackets. But if a work has artistic merit now—if it's not just written for lascivious values alone—legally you can pretty much say anything you damn please. Of course, this new book of mine is bound to be banned as obscene in Boston. What isn't?"

After its publication, *The Grapes of Wrath* was banned from the library in Pacific Grove, the town where it was mainly written, and it was twice burned publicly in Salinas. It also achieved the provocative honor of being the most banned book in all the high schools of America. I don't recall whether or not it was banned in Boston, but the furor was horrendous everywhere.

The publication of *Grapes of Wrath*, in 1939, brought John new recognition, notoriety, and wealth—the three things in the world he always said he didn't want. *Grapes*, to most readers, was a disturbing and shocking book, but I felt it was by far the best thing he'd ever written. I couldn't find one word in it I would have changed—certainly not the Controversial Word, itself.

Life in Los Gatos, for the Steinbecks, had become more and more untenable. The new house they built next to Jean's uncle's ranch, had been practically under siege. There'd been mountains of mail, much of it vituperative, most of it crank letters begging him for money, or for support for this or that wild-eyed cause. The Steinbecks sold their new house, and moved further out into the hills, to a secluded ranch near a Trappist monastery and a long narrow lake. John and Carol temporarily lived in the old farmhouse on the property while building their new ranch-style place nearby. When it was completed they moved in and used the original farmhouse to house their occasional guests. Few knew the location of their new layout, and the Steinbecks had no telephone.

There was an old well on the property that John said seemed to be bottomless. He dropped a stone down it. We listened and, sure enough, there was no returning sound.

"I'd like to heave all the bastards that are pestering me down there," he said sourly.

I remembered that rather ridiculous incident in Gus Gay's garden, the day before we'd gone to Baja, only three years earlier—the time that John had put on the dark glasses to avoid the fluttering old ladies. That seemed like a children's game of charades now, by comparison. Besides, John and Carol's constant quarreling was getting worse, and I was sure Carol was drinking more than was good for her. Money, once their major worry, seemed to be the only problem they didn't have these days. Twentieth Century Fox bought *Grapes* for seventy-five grand, reportedly the highest price ever for a book to that date. *Mice and Men* had been made into a fine movie, starring Lon Chaney, Jr. and Burgess Meredith, as Lenny and George. It was playing to packed houses around the world. John's name had become box office magic in filmland and there was much talk of even bigger productions to come. Steinbeck was spending increasingly more time in Hollywood, away from Carol and the Los Gatos ranch. He batched in at the Garden of Allah, where F. Scott Fitzgerald had once lived. There'd been talk of tearing down the old stucco buildings, so John moved to a more modern and private apartment nearby at the Aloha.

About this time John met Gwendolyn Conger, "a friend of a friend" who, as I first heard it from Ed, was a plump and pretty little cabaret torch-singer who was working off and on as a movie extra. The girl said she was twenty-one, but after Ed first met her he told us she looked dangerously younger, maybe even under eighteen.

John was at a time in his life when he was restless, at loose ends, and in that susceptible forty-ish age sometimes referred to as the period of the seven year itch. For John, seeing Gwyn for the first time must have been like a burst of sunlight. She was a charmer. She had honey-colored hair and a flawless magnolia blossom complexion. She, in turn, must have been greatly impressed by his craggy bulk, his colorful conversation, his famous name and, unquestionably, by the fact that he obviously had lots of money.

Several times Jean and I had gone to college dances at The Fairmont in San Fransisco, before we were married. We'd been similarly charmed there by a teen-aged singer and dancer named Betty Grable. She'd been so young, delicious, and starry-eyed that she took The City by storm, just as she later did Hollywood and the world. When John first met Gwyn, I fancy she hit him the same way Grable did the college boys. Though we didn't meet Gwyn until some time after she married John, I thought then she resembled Grable and she probably had, even more so, when she first met John. Ed kept us up to date on their developing affair.

Actually, Ed was always more our friend than John was—which was true for everyone in the Lab group, I'm sure. John had sworn Ed to secrecy on many of the things that Ed later told us. Ed was too honest or ingenuous ever to keep a secret well. John found himself caught between Gwyn and Carol. It was a ferocious triangle full of accusations and in-fighting. According to Ed both women claimed to be pregnant, but he didn't believe either of them were. It was just another "trick to catch the Old One" as the early quote had it, about trying to trap the Devil himself. Ed told us a lot more, and swore us to secrecy in turn, and though Ed's been dead for well over a quarter of a century, I'll try to honor that request. At least on most of the details that haven't already been reported. Suffice it to say that John and Carol were divorced, that John and Gwyn were married some time later in New Orleans, and that the newlyweds thereafter lived in New York City.

The rumor going around town was that John, in order to get out of his old marriage and into his new one, had given Carol a settlement of a half million dollars in cold cash. Carol vehemently denied it. She said it was more like a fifth of that. It has since been published that it was more than twice what Carol told us. Even so, one hundred grand was very big bucks in those days, though currently, in Monterey, that much would scarcely buy the average small two-bedroom bungalow. Carol told us she intended to invest the money wisely, and I believe she did. She always pinched the pennies and shell-gamed their finances, all the time she and John had been eeking with the rest of us in the early days of the Depression. After the divorce, Carol started running around with the Fort Ord army officer set. Soon after, we heard she married a lieutenant somewhat younger than she, who'd been a "gentleman cowboy" in civilian life.

Carol and Jean had always been good friends. They saw eye to eye on most subjects, such as literature and politics. They were both early examples of today's liberated woman. Jean's adroitness at topping John's lines amused Carol. She said she wished she could have done it as well, instead of always blowing her fuse and giving John a good cussing out in front of everyone.

In the first days after the divorce, Carol had been very bitter about John's "ratting out" on her. She said so all around town without any inhibitions. She said she felt like the proverbial trained nurse who'd worked her ass off to put her husband through medical school to get his degree, only to have him ditch her for his first good-looking debutante patient.

There was no question in our minds that Carol had been responsible for much, if not most, of John's success. As Jean put it, Carol had "goosed John up the ladder of fame by his bootstraps." All their married life Carol had worked at a series of low-paying, boring jobs to make enough so John could stay home and write. She performed all the traditional housewifely tasks, too, on both weekends and weeknights after coming home from work. She shopped, cooked, washed, cleaned, made love, and, in addition, she edited and typed John's manuscripts, and made them ready for mailing to the publishers. Fortunately, she seemed to have endless good health and energy. I never made a sketch of her. She seemed to be on wires, always full of movement. She would never sit still that long for me, or for anyone—or for anything.

I thought she was a damned good editor, too. She groomed John's sometimes sloppy and sentimental prose with a steel-bristled, intellectual, curry comb. After the divorce, there was a marvelous story going around the Lab that illustrated this point.

Pat Covici was John's soft-spoken, well-tailored publisher from New York. He'd been a consistent booster for John, who, of course, was to reward him very well by becoming his best best-selling author. Pat came out to the Lab several times over the years. He observed us all somewhat curiously, if not clinically, I thought. It seemed that, after Ed's death, John was having trouble with his

Monterey Boat Works — China Point   Bruce Ariss 1937

second marriage and, as always, he was trying to solve his personal problems by throwing hard work over them. He dug in, writing voluminously on his new "big book" on Salinas Valley. When Pat Covici received *East of Eden* he was said to have been appalled by its length and formlessness. In desperation, he flew out to the West Coast and asked Carol if she could bring herself to let bygones be bygones and edit John's meandering manuscript into some sort of disciplined shape. With a few indelicate words, Carol had told him to go take a flying jump at the moon.

To give John some credit, it had not been as easy as it appeared for him to walk out on Carol. He was fond of her and, as he said, they'd been though a hell of a lot together. He felt remorse and guilt, and I think he was genuinely sorry for all the rage and grief he was causing her. They never had any kids, probably because John always proclaimed that his art must come first. Carol had always gone along with that. Perhaps, if they'd had children, they might have stayed together for that reason alone, but I rather doubt it. Their rift was too great, and his sudden infatuation for Gwyn was overpowering.

The wrangling went on for weeks. John was so upset about the whole mess that he said he couldn't sleep or write anymore. He commissioned Ellwood Graham, the young artist whose studio was next to mine on The Hill, to paint his portrait. Ellwood's pretty wife, Barbara, was also a fine painter. She sat in on the session and painted a second portrait of John, strictly for her own satisfaction.

John hadn't been able to get anywhere on the book about the extensive sea voyage he made to Baja in the previous year, in 1940, which was to result in a collaboration with Ed. It was long overdue at the publishers. He took the opportunity while sitting for the portraits to go over his notes and the ship's log book to put together the *Sea of Cortez*, which was published later that year, in 1941.

This expedition was made by boat in the spring of 1940, exactly four years after the land trip we made along the west coast of Baja. John was financing the trip, and Carol was going along as cook.

A premonition? My block cut cover for the Pine Cone — 5 days before WW II

It was a spartan, working-type voyage, on a seventy-five foot converted purse seiner, the *Western Flyer*. The captain, Tony Berry, was from Seattle. There was three principals, Ed, John, and Carol, plus Tex Travis as engineer. Two local fishermen, Sparkey Anea and Tony Colletto, were signed on as deck hands.

The Lab group went down to Fisherman's Wharf and saw them off. The boat rode low in the water and looked awfully small to me. It was a hot day on the Wharf. Carol, in a skimpy blue sunsuit, was cross, sweating profusely, and trying to get out a meal in the crowded galley. There was quite a celebration going on, and Toby Street was going along as far as San Diego. We saw them off with great whoops and hollers.

I'd walked into the studio next door several times while John was posing—and composing. I thought he looked terrible. His pale eyes and big nose were red and swollen. He looked like he'd been weeping which, Barbara told me later, he had been. She thought John was on the verge of a nervous breakdown from all the stress and strain he was under from his furious triangle.

I thought Ellwood's painting of John was great. It caught all the turmoil he was undergoing and captured the hunted look in his eyes. I thought Ellwood had made John look like Lenny in *Of Mice and Men*, just as he was about to tell George that if he wasn't appreciated, he would go off into the hills and live in a cave. I ran a full-color, full-page reproduction of the portrait in my magazine, sometime later.

Naturally Carol hated the portrait, just as she hated my Mexican sketch of John. She said she wouldn't have it in the house. Ed hung it in a place of honor in his Lab, right over the turntable of his custom-built phonograph. The portrait that Barbara painted of John was more complimentary and I'm sure would have been acceptable to Carol, but that wasn't the portrait they'd paid for. After Ed died, John gave Ellwood's painting to Burgess Meredith, who had become one of John's closest friends.

I heard that John had persuaded Burgess and Ed to form an independent company with him to film *Cannery Row*. John wanted the former to play the latter, that is, Burgess to play Ed, which would have been excellent casting. Burgess was about the same size and general appearance as Ed, and was a fine actor. With a beard and a little makeup he would have been perfect as "Doc." Unfortunately, the show never materialized. John said that a former agent of his in Hollywood had filed a "million dollar nuisance suit," claiming he still owned the film rights. John said the agent had originally decided the book could never be made into a film and had sent it back. John apparently hadn't bothered to secure a written release from their original agreement, so they were in trouble. He could have settled for a smaller flat sum, out of court, which was probably all the agent had expected, but John, feeling this would be like paying blackmail, angrily cancelled the whole project instead. Too bad it didn't go through.

Recently, at a Steinbeck commemorative in Salinas, Jean and I met Burgess Meredith again. We asked him what had happened to Ellwood Graham's portrait Steinbeck had given him. He told us a mutual good friend of his and John's—John Huston, the director—had talked him out of the picture one time when he was in a weak moment.

I enjoyed being editor of a new monthly magazine called—of all things—*What's Doing on The Monterey Peninsula*. My two assistant editors were Toby Street's imperious blonde second wife, Peggy, and Ed Ricketts' handsome and intelligent girlfriend, Toni Siexas Jackson. Toni was also John's secretary when he was in Monterey, and had done much of the typing for him that Carol used to do before their divorce. Because of these inside connections, our little local magazine often scooped the world on John's current literary projects.

In the March 1947 issue of *What's Doing* I ran a full-page color reproduction of Ellwood Graham's craggy portrait of John. On the facing page I ran Toni's review of his latest novel, *The Wayward Bus*, his second post-war book. Toni had gone East to do the typing on this book since John had sold his Monterey adobe and was now settled securely in New York. Toni thought this new novel was a great work of art. She classed it somewhere between *Of Mice and Men* and *The Grapes of Wrath*.

The third book of John's to be published after the war was *The Pearl*. Although he'd been thinking about this yarn since before the war—he heard it at La Paz while aboard the *Western Flyer* on the 1940 Baja trip to the Sea of Cortez—he placed it on a back burner. He'd been too busy on wartime projects and going overseas as a foreign correspondent to think much about it. When he finally got back to it, *The Pearl* proved to be a well-crafted short novel about a simple Mexican fisherman who found a "pearl of great price" that almost destroyed his life.

My most satisfying acting role at the two Wharf Theaters (both of which I helped design and build) was that of Lenny, the retarded giant in Steinbeck's *Of Mice and Men*. It was the same piece of work that—a decade and a half earlier on the beach in Baja—I told its author it was "interesting, but would never sell." After such an error in judgement there's no doubt in my mind that that was why I'd won the role of the big moron in the play—I was typecast for it. Everyone in our little cast hoped John would come out to our production of his play, the first one in his home area, but I told them it wasn't likely. John hadn't even gone to the original big Broadway opening of *Mice and Men* a decade earlier. In spite of its long and successful run in New York he made a point of not going to see it, for reasons unknown to anyone, probably even to himself.

About this time my little magazine and I became embroiled in a journalistic battle with the giant *San Francisco Examiner*. They had reported the existence of a so-called "Sex Cult" that had been established in the Big Sur area by the notorious author, Henry Miller. It sounded phony to me. I'd known Henry pretty well for years and it didn't make any sense. I went down to check it out and found there was no such thing. It was all a hoax. I said so in the next issue of my magazine and was immediately branded by the Hearst papers as "The Barker for the Big Sur Sex Cult."

Reporters and weirdos flocked into the Big Sur to write about, or join the cult, but since it didn't exist, it soon blew over. I wrote a three-act comedy about the incident which I produced for the Wharf Theater. Henry Miller came to see it and said he thoroughly enjoyed it. My play got so much publicity in the California papers that a scout from MGM encouraged me to come down with it to see if it could be made into a movie.

I spent the next five years commuting weekly from Monterey to Hollywood, mainly working in the art departments of the major studios. I was at MGM when its president, Dore Schary, called me to tell me he loved my play, but couldn't use it because there was too much sex in it. This was in 1951 when movies were being rigidly censored. A cute little comedy, *The Moon Is Blue*, had just been banned because the heroine had used the word pregnant.

Steinbeck's exalted literary stature gave him quite an advantage in the film business. He was freed from most of the commercial pressures Hollywoods puts on screenwriters. His name was a big box office draw, and he knew it. He could demand more favorable agreements from the studios than other writers could, particularly in regards to changes in his scripts. However, in the late 1940s while I was in Hollywood, I heard rumors about his big battle with the English producer-director, Alfred Hitchcock.

John had been hired by 20th Century Fox to do the screenplay for the film, *Lifeboat*. After the movie was released, John discovered that the script had been altered. At Hitchcock's request, they hired another writer to change it all around. The character of the black sailor in the boat had been radically changed. He had become a racial stereotype and treated in a derogatory fashion. To add insult to injury, the picture turned out to have anti-labor overtones which, of course, was entirely foreign to Steinbeck's philosophy. Steinbeck was outraged. He tried to have his name taken off the credits, but without success. He'd been hired to write, so his script was considered a commercial product belonging to the producer to do with what he pleased. The film was billed on movie marquees across the nation as JOHN STEINBECK'S *LIFEBOAT*. Like many another lesser author in the film capital, Steinbeck learned the hard way that the screenwriter's role is considered little more than that of a "producer's lead pencil."

But, in general, Steinbeck came out ahead in Hollywood, a place infamous for chewing up and spitting out creative people. For one thing, the box office appeal of his name was almost certifiable at the bank. It gave him an enormous and unprecedented leverage over the petty tyrants who ran the industry. He was one of the very few there who could stand up for his rights and get away with it.

For example, he told Daryl Zanuck (who was popularly known as the King of the Talent Eaters) that he was putting aside the $75,000 he'd been paid for *Grapes of Wrath* until after the picture was finished. If his work was watered down, or distorted in any way, he would use the money to "sue the pants off" the producers.

His threat worked. His epic motion picture on the plight of the downtrodden Dust Bowl gypsies was as authentic as a black and white documentary. In Hollywood, Steinbeck became an overnight hero to all the thousands of motion picture people who had been crushed under the juggernaut cog wheels of those gigantic studio cameras.

John was in and out of 20th Century Fox, primarily working on *Viva Zapata!*, for most of the years I was in Hollywood. He had also worked with that studio on *The Grapes of Wrath*, which had won him the Academy Award.

It seemed to me that John had been on that Zapata script forever. It never seemed to satisfy him and he kept changing it. I'd remembered him sweating over it, back in Pacific Grove, and that was years ago. He'd told me that he wanted it to be an absolutely accurate portrayal of the great Mexican revolutionary hero, but he didn't think Hollywood would let him get away with it. They seemed to have an unwritten rule in the movies that you couldn't do anything that was accurate! He'd managed to wrangle quite a bit of studio money to pay for his private research. He showed me sheaves of neatly typed reports, and depositions from the contemporaries of Zapata who were still alive. I supposed he'd become so lost in the maze of all those elaborate details that he couldn't find his way out.

In 1952 I was working as a production designer at Selznick's old studio in Culver City, which had been taken over by RKO after Selznick had gone broke on *Portrait of Jenny*. The top spot for designers in those days was the Stanley Kramer Unit at Columbia, and I was hoping to get on there. I struck up an acquaintance with Rudy Sternad, Kramer's head designer, and I was waiting for a promised job with him soon.

Through a weird set of coincidences this was to affect the future of Cannery Row. Rudy happened to mention that Kramer was unhappy with the Hollywood scene, and wanted to get away from it all and do fine art films somewhere where there was peace and quiet.

"I know just the place," I told him. "Old Cannery Row

"Salvage"

in Monterey is defunct. It's filled with big empty buildings that could easily be converted into sound stages. They're built out half over the water, so they'd have to be pretty heavily insulated to block out the sound of the surf, but that shouldn't be too much trouble. Most stages have to be insulated for airplanes going overhead, anyway."

"Sounds great!" Rudy said. "I'll talk to Kramer and get back to you." Sternad called me into his office soon after.

"Kramer likes the idea. Here's what he wants you to do. Locate a reliable real estate broker, preferably a good friend of yours. Have him do a search for all the owners of canneries that seem adequate, sizewise. But this all has to be done in strictest confidence. Don't let anyone know who's behind the inquiries. Otherwise the prices will go out of sight. Can you do it?"

"I think so. Yeah. I think I know just the man. Nick Nickele, of Preble and Nickele Realty in Monterey. He's a nice young guy who feels he owes me a favor. Indirectly, I got him a lot of amusing publicity recently in the *New Yorker*. I wrote a tongue in cheek ad for him about an artist's studio on Huckleberry Hill that was for sale. I said the prospective purchaser would have to bring samples of his art work, or his writing, to see if it was good enough, before he could buy the studio. A *New Yorker* writer, S.J. Perelman, somehow read the ad. He was so amused that he sat down and wrote a hypothetical short story about artists and writers being interviewed by Preble and Nickele. It was called "Monet Makes the World Go Round," and when it was published Nickele had a lot of fun and some business out of it, too, I guess. I'm sure he'd do the job for us, and keep it under his hat."

On my next weekend home I talked to young Nick and he eagerly agreed to go along with the secret project. After all, if it went through, there'd be some pretty big commissions ahead for him. In a couple of weeks of hard digging Nick searched out the names of the owners of most of the big abandoned canneries.

I never met Kramer. As usual, in Hollywood, you always dealt with go-betweens, but sometime later Sternad got back to me again. Kramer had checked everything out, but had discovered a hitch. He always reviewed the daily rushes before the next day's shooting, Sternad said. If the film were to be shot in Cannery Row, it would have to be flown to the L. A. photolabs to be processed that night, in order to get it back before the following morning. There were no evening flights from the Monterey airport, so the whole scheme was out of the question.

Then the negative news. Sternad said later that apparently Kramer had been right about one thing. Just the fact that a mysterious someone was interested, had set everybody on the Row speculating. A company had been quickly formed to buy up as many of the old canneries as possible for their eventual use as restaurants and gift shops. The new Cannery Row was off and running on a new track.

I was just as happy the movie deal hadn't gone through. Kramer with his art films might have been okay, but there probably would have been a related influx of oversized motion picture outfits that wouldn't have been. I'd quit my Chamber of Commerce style magazine partly because it was bringing in too much tourism. A big busy movie industry might have proved just as bad, or worse, for the Peninsula's ecology.

Fortunately, I escaped from Hollywood soon afterward. I heard that Bing Crosby was opening a new TV station, right in Monterey. I landed the job of supervisor on the strength of having worked on the "I Love Lucy" show which had now become the number one rated series in the nation. I didn't mention that "Lucy" was not strictly a television production. (Desi Arnez, to avoid going to New York to shoot live TV, had come up with the bright idea of using three regular Hollywood 35mm movie cameras, in an imitation of the TV style, and filming the action before a live studio audience.) It didn't much matter, because at that time nobody else knew anything about television, either. It was all a ham operation.

Bing Crosby was the best boss I'd ever worked for. Once a year, in January, at the time of the annual Crosby Gold Tournament in nearby Pebble Beach, he'd wander in, say,

"Howzit goin'?" and breeze right out again. I settled back home in Monterey, expecting a long happy career as a television executive.

That didn't happen, either. Some three years later, when everything was running like clockwork, Bing's first wife, Dixie, died quite suddenly. Crosby was stuck with a huge tax bill from the government. Apparently, California was a community property state, which meant he had to pay inheritance taxes on half of everything he owned. Which was a lot. In cash, and right now! He sold the Monterey station to Salinas. There went my nice, lifelong job! Bing moved to Nevada, and I found a job as an art director in an ad agency in the San Francisco area.

I was back commuting weekends again, hating it, and watching for a job in Monterey. One eventually came, and I was working at home again, this time for Hank Ketcham, drawing "Dennis the Menace" for his monthly comic magazine. Sometime later, I accidentally fell into a steady, pleasant but somewhat lower paying job as an illustrator of foreign language texts, right next door at the Presidio on Huckleberry Hill.

By now, our three oldest kids were all in college at the same time and finances were becoming a distinct problem. Jean and I had always felt that money was only for spending, so we seemed to be broke all the time. To augment the college fund, Jean decided to go back to work as a writer, of novels this time, since she'd never had much luck selling her short stories. Besides, TV was replacing magazines, and short stories just weren't selling, period. Surprisingly, her first two novels were accepted and published to world-wide critical acclaim. Reviewers said these were great modern classics and everyone should be forced to read them. Apparently, this was the kiss of death because, as usual, the public was only buying novels that critics said were such trash that no one should be allowed to read them. Jean didn't make too much money, but what she did make helped, and her two fine novels brought her prestige in literary circles.

The Quick Years, her first novel, was published in England. Payment came, not in pounds sterling, but in guineas, perhaps because the class-conscious British believed that professional authors should be paid in a special kind of royal currency. They also believed that a healthy bite should be taken out of her check for the Queen's Tax.

Elizabeth Bowen, London's leading literary critic, was ecstatic over Jean's book. She said Jean wrote like a combination of D.H. Lawrence, G.B. Sterne, Jack London, and John Steinbeck at his best.

"I hope John doesn't read that one," I told Jean. "He'll go out of his mind. He was always irritated with you for topping him in arguments. Now this. Exactly the kind of unqualified rave review he always hoped for on his own books, but never got.

"What good are raves?" Jean said. "I'd gladly trade all of them for one of John's monthly royalty checks. Besides, I don't guess he'll see any of my reviews. He told me he religiously never reads any reviews. Ever."

I said I rather doubted that would be possible, since a stunning Russ Cummings photo of Jean's classic profile had been all over the country's newspaper reviewing pages, and another by Spike Graham had appeared in *Time* magazine. Sometime later we learned from a young writer friend of ours that Jean's guess had been correct. Dennis Murphy, whose family had been neighbors of the Steinbeck family in Salinas, wrote a fine first novel called *The Sergeant*. We heard that John had helped him get it published. Dennis had gone back to New York, staying with John at his East Side apartment.

One morning at breakfast, Dennis asked John if he'd heard that Jean Ariss had a new book out. Dennis told us that John had choked on a mouthful of coffee and turned livid.

"Any book that gal has written about me is a goddamned lie!" Steinbeck had managed to sputter out through a spray of hot coffee.

Dennis had reported this scene to us with unconcealed amusement. I remarked that perhaps John had been thunderstruck at the thought of some of the confessions he'd spilled out over the years about his personal problems. When John had been in pain, physically or emotionally, like a half-butchered bull calf, he'd not been exactly reticent about it. Dennis said he'd assured John that there was absolutely nothing about him in either of Jean's books. John may have been reassured, but whether he was curious enough to read Jean's books or not, we never discovered.

Over the years I must have painted almost a hundred big murals in the Monterey area, but generally they've had a relatively short life. Public buildings or restaurants close down or burn down. Hotels paint out murals when they redecorate. John was in one of my bar murals. He and Toby Street practically held court in front of the designs, wherein John was depicted as a scrubby-looking musician in an old Wild West Saloon. He was banging on the piano while Toby played the guitar and sang with his head back and his mouth wide open.

I was asked to redesign a whole town—Jolon, down in South Monterey County. It was out in the empty back country of Monterey, in a world that John had described so well in his early books about pioneer settlers in the far reaches of a county so huge that it's roughly three times the size of the State of Rhode Island, but with less than a third the population. John's folks had shipped him to Jolon when he was a kid, to recuperate from a near-death bout with pneumonia.

When I finally got home to Huckleberry Hill all my friends were missing. I felt strangely like Rip Van Winkle. Curious, I asked around, until I eventually discovered they were all at a funeral.

Ed Ricketts had been killed. His old car had been smashed by the Del Monte Express at a blind crossing on Cannery Row. Poor Ed, in the hospital, had been badly crushed by the engine and lingered on for days while his many friends crowded into the waiting room. He finally died from his internal injuries.

The funeral was already over. I missed it by several hours. I went searching for Jean. Someone said she was down at John's old place on Eleventh Street. John had flown out from New York, and had barely made it in time for the funeral, himself.

Jean said later she didn't see John go in to the service, which was held in the little chapel out the by the lighthouse, but he joined a group of them later (among others, Milt and Betsy Heifitz, Ed's new wife Alice, and Jean), to sit in silence out on the rocks and watch the Pacific Ocean breaking out beyond Ed's beloved tidepools.

Jean hadn't been dressed to go to a funeral. She was wearing her usual jeans and tee shirt, and hadn't gone in with the others.

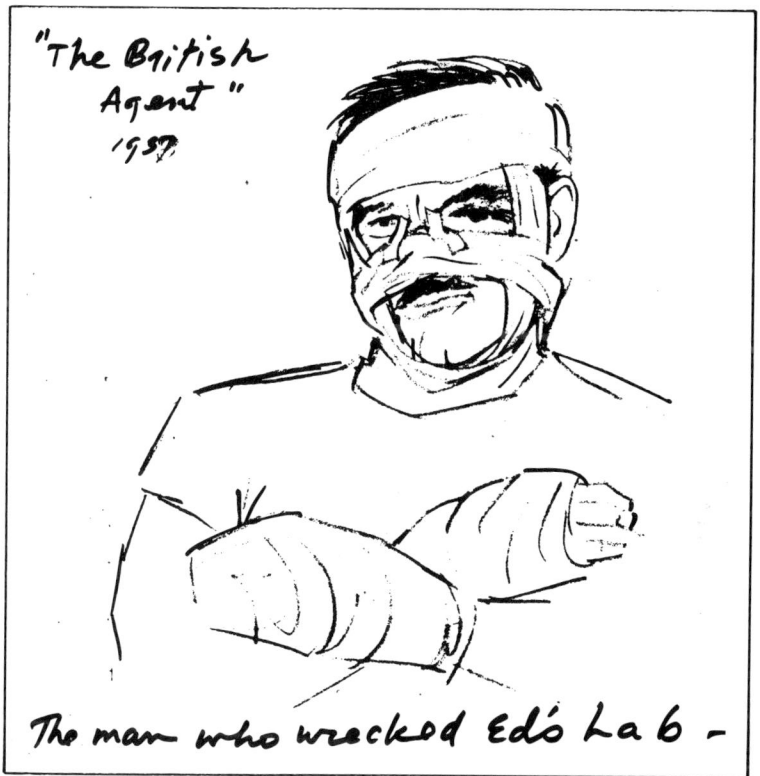

"The British Agent" 1957

The man who wrecked Ed's Lab -

"That's all right," John had reassured her. "I'm sure Ed wouldn't go to his funeral either, if he could help it."

It was dusk when I drove up to John's house. The gate was locked. I rattled the cowbell suspended from it. John shuffled out though the side garden, looking surprisingly old and stooped in the fading light.

"I just heard about Ed," I said. "God, what a shock! Is Jean here?"

"Yeah. Yeah, it's been terrible, all right. Come on in." He carefully locked the gate again after I was inside. "Jean and I have been going over Ed's papers. You should have telephoned ahead."

"What? How could I? I mean, your place has been closed up, so I figured you wouldn't have a phone, or you'd have a new unlisted number, or something."

"No, no! It's not unlisted. It's right in the book. When we get inside the house I'll show you."

"That's okay. I believe you." I stopped myself from saying anything more. He wasn't making any sense. Here was a guy who was always complaining about his lack of privacy, and he tells me he lists his phone number in the public telephone book! I wondered if he had both his oars in the water. As we reached the dim light from the French doors that opened into his living room, I noticed he was carrying a huge horse pistol, almost two feet long, in his right hand.

"What's the gun for?" I asked in surprise.

"You can't be too careful, nowadays!" John rolled his eyes around to look back over his shoulder into the shadowy garden and added darkly, "How was I to know who was ringing my bell?"

He looked ridiculous, standing there with the big pistol dangling in his hand. I stared at him in disbelief. What the hell was the matter with him? I knew John had always been something of a gun nut, but now he was sounding positively paranoid. Admittedly, he'd been living in New York City for the past few years—the asphalt jungle, and all that—but Pacific Grove in 1948 had no crime problems. Most people here didn't bother to lock their doors, day or night, or even when they were away from home for a day or two.

I felt a sudden feeling of exasperation. To me, John's off-beat behavior had a strange, surrealistic quality about it. Was Ed's death proving too much for him? Was it self-pity, or was he just dramatizing his grief for my benefit? In the night air around me I could almost hear the voice of Ed, his faithful apologist, saying gently, as he had so often before when he was alive, "Well, you know, John is just being John."

Jean and John had been reading stacks of Ed's papers

they brought up from the Lab. Jean told me later that John had been flinging stuff into the fire that he said was too personal to save—notes about people we all knew. Ed had always been a conscientiously detailed diarist, but Jean suspected John was also burning a lot of material that might disclose how important Ed's thinking had been to his own development as a writer. John had become overly protective of his literary reputation these days, Jean felt, but there wasn't much she could do about his wholesale act of pyromania.

John poured me a shot of straight whiskey and the three of us sipped at the glasses of liquor while we contemplated the flames. John suggested that Jean and he might collaborate on a book about Ed. Jean said no, she couldn't write that way. John said yeah, he just about decided he couldn't write with anyone, either.

Jean mentioned that Ed had dropped by to see her last week. He'd been expecting to go on another expedition—the boat trip he planned with John—to the Queen Charlotte Islands, off British Columbia. If anything should happen to him, Ed had said rather unexpectedly, would Jean look after his new wife, Alice? She was very young and inexperienced. Jean said of course, but thought it rather odd he should say such a thing. Now she wondered if he might have had a premonition that something like this was going to happen to him.

Ed had always been psychic about such things. The three of us began recalling Ed's other unusual qualities. What a profound influence he had on everyone he knew! We agreed that his death would be, to all of us on Cannery Row, the end of an era.

Ed's dark-haired wife, Alice, was a quiet, slender, Irish-looking girl. After the funeral she learned from Toby that her marriage to Ed had not been legal. Ed hadn't picked up, or signed, the divorce papers from his first marriage. The divorce hadn't gone through. Apparently he had presumed his first wife had taken care of everything. Toby said there wasn't anything that could be done about it. The next day Alice quietly departed for her hometown, somewhere in the Central Valley. Steinbeck went back to New York, but since he owned the note on the Lab, he soon after sold the place to Jack Yee, a Cannery Row landlord, who was the owner of the Wing Chong grocery store building across the street.

Life went on, but we all missed those good social evenings at the Lab. An English teacher at the high school. a bachelor named Harlan Watkins, rented the Lab for his residence. I think it gave him quite a bit of prestige with his creative writing classes. Some years later, just before he married and moved out, Harlan came up with a brilliant idea. Why not form a men's club and buy the old building to preserve it from destruction, and then maintain it as a sort of literary monument? Twenty of us, mostly artists and professional men, chipped in and purchased it for a modest price. Today, due to Harlan's inspiration, the gatherings at the Lab are going on, after all.

During and after the war, Steinbeck, with his strong ties to Monterey, had actually made a number of attempts to settle in here with his second wife, Gwyn, but like Thomas Wolfe, he was already feeling "you can't go home again." Personally, I think he didn't want to go home again. He had pretty much joined the jet set by this time. I told Jean I thought his international travels and recognition had keyed him up to a life far beyond our peninsular one. He tried several times, but he just couldn't fit back into our small puddle.

Gwyn simply wasn't interested in trying. She felt all of John's old friends had also been old friends of Carol's and would be sitting around in judgement of her. Her tinselly Hollywood background probably made her feel out of place, too. She'd discovered that Southern California and Northern California were as unalike as two separate countries in Europe. In spite of all the rather bizarre and exciting occurrences that seemed to be going on around us, Gwyn was bored. Like the blasé old gentleman in the vintage movie, she had already made up her mind that "Nothing ever happens in the Grand Hotel."

Jean felt it was quite the opposite. She said, even if she

just sat at home and minded her own business, she was still the victim of a continuous stream of unlikely visitors and strange involvements.

Once, for example, a former Mexican senator talked her into letting him use our upstairs studio for his headquarters in order to hatch an international revolution. Jean thought it might make good material for a book. There were FBI and CIA people watching our house night and day.

It had all been news to me. I found out about it when I came home from a few months work in Big Sur, where I was a construction straw boss on a big monastery job. That weekend, as a sort of lark, I'd brought home an enormously fat valet for myself. He was a down-and-out gentleman's gentleman, an alcoholic, who ended up trying to dry out by working for me on my crew of laborers for the monks. As a construction worker, of course, he was a joke. Terribly miscast. He wore a beautifully tailored double-breasted gray suit, a Homburg hat, spats, and gray kid gloves. I put him to digging post holes with a double handled digger, which he did ineffectively and with great delicacy. After the first day, he wanted to go back to the City. He fastened on to me because he'd heard I had a big house in Monterey. He said he'd act as my valet without pay. Only board and room (The way he ate I was sure he'd make a good salary for himself doing only that!). He was very persistent. He'd be a great help. He'd answer the doorbell (we didn't have one) and take the visitors' cards to me on a silver salver (we didn't have one of those either). If I didn't wish to see the visitors, he'd usher them right out. He said that was his specialty.

I thought it was so delightfully incongruous that I told him I'd take him home for a trial weekend. I thought it might amuse Jean. When we stepped inside my front door, two villainous-looking armed guards slammed us up against the wall and frisked us for weapons.

"What the hell's going on here?" I demanded angrily.
"Who are you?"
"I live here! I own this place. Who the hell are you?"
"Oh, you must be Mister Bruce! Sorry, Señor! Come right in." In heavy accents they explained about the revolution being hatched upstairs in my studio.

I turned to glance at my fat valet friend. His face was white with fear, and he was just disappearing out the door. My staunch gentleman's gentleman, the very same one who had promised to demand visiting cards before letting anyone near me, was off and pounding down the road as fast as his fat legs could carry him.

"Hey! Wait up!" I yelled after him. "You forgot to get these guys' calling cards!" I never saw him again.

The Mexican revolution never quite materialized. Although Jean took took down the Senator's dictation, transformed it into ringing Jeffersonian phrases, and copies of the Manifesto that she wrote for them were distributed and read before the United Nations in New York, it was all at the wrong time.

President Kennedy was on the eve of a Good Neighbor visit to Mexico and the State Department immediately squelched any action on the movement.

I'm afraid I was delighted to hear it. The revolutionists in my studio had become a great bore and I felt their idolatry of Jean had become positively maudlin. Over toasts of red wine they announced that after their success they would put up a statue of her in Mexico City as the noble Mother of the Revolution. They even talked of a triumphant entry into the capital by parachute, with Jean descending beside them amongst flying flags and flowers.

When one of the upstairs revolutionists went home for a weekend in Los Angeles and was assassinated on a street corner, I said enough is enough! Next thing, I figured, these characters would be shooting at each other over our kids' heads. I ushered them all out and that was the last I ever heard of their crazy revolution.

Perhaps that was the most melodramatic incident on the Hill at that period, but there were others going on nearly every day. Another time I answered a polite knock at my door to let in a sweet little old Helen Hokinson *New Yorker* type lady. She was carrying a stack of magazines neatly tied with a pink ribbon.

"My name is Mrs. Joe Doaks," she said demurely. "I'm

moving from my home in Carmel Valley after my dear husband's recent death. I found these marvelous magazines that you edited, and I couldn't bring myself to throw them out. So I've brought them to you."

I thanked her kindly then realized her mouth had fallen open. I'd been working on a painting and had oil colors all over my hands, and probably on my face, too, but it wasn't that. She was staring at the collection of people in my big living room. Over by the fireplace, a rock preacher was performing the marriage ceremony for two young jazz singer acquaintances of ours. He was accompanying himself on the guitar as he sang the wedding service in a hillbilly nasal. At one end of our slab-door dining table a bearded orthodox Jewish editor friend of mine from New York was performing a Friday night candle-light blessing. He wore a white Palm Beach suit on his short plump figure with an embroidered prayer shawl draped over his shoulders. A matching yarmulke was perched atop his black curls. He was chanting in a deep monotone through his heavy curling black beard. His tall handsome wife, who didn't happen to be Jewish, was ignoring him completely, warming her broad backside in front of the nearby wall heater, her hands clasped behind her. She was dressed in a loose-fitting striped gown. It looked like a circus tent, because she was approximately nine months pregnant. She was watching the hill-billy marriage ceremony very intently, as was the month-old kitten that had stuck its head out of the generous cleavage she displayed from her low-cut bodice.

One of my pre-teen aged daughters, in a pale blue tou-tou, was practicing high knee ballet steps to a muted recording of *Oklahoma!* At the other end of the slab-table Jean was typing away at one of her short stories. She had learned absolute concentration. She'd been raised in a family of six kids, now had five of her own, with six more of her sister's children, from next door, in and out of the house at all times of the day. She could keep right on typing and never hear the telephone ringing itself off its cradle three feet away from her head. The whole scene was strictly out of that mad hatter's comedy, *You Can't Take It With You.*

WAR WORK: The Artist as Catskinner — 1944.

Mrs. Joe Doaks gulped, trying to think of something polite to say. She noticed the kids' oversized yellow tomcat (named Charley, "because he was as big as a horse") dozing imperturbably on the lazy susan in the center of the table.

"Well," Mrs. Doaks said. "I see you have a very nice cat!" She made a sudden panicky dash for the door.

Over the years, our studio had gradually become a sort of Bohemian waystation for the West Coast, a point of transfer for all the artists, writers, musicians, alcoholics, intellectuals, geniuses, and other diverse crackpots on their way through Central California. I must confess, that in expansive moods, I'd invited most of them home, but they usually brought their own uninvited friends along with them.

Jean said I should have been a Southern Colonel, the master of an old antebellum plantation. The problem was, she pointed out, that I didn't have a dozen slaves to do the housework—only herself. Jean eventually became a little tired of the scene, perhaps because she was the only one cooking the dinners, setting the table, and washing the dishes for a daily dozen or more. She seemed to do it all so effortlessly and so graciously that I couldn't see why she complained about it. I thought the majority of our guests were marvelous characters, and only rarely did I have to do the bouncer act and throw one of them out. I felt that, if Jean wanted to be a great writer, she really should meet a variety of interesting people.

Eventually, I admit, it got out of hand. We'd invite a couple dozen people to a party and a couple hundred would show up. Columnists from the San Francisco papers would come down to check out our gatherings. Dr. Eric Berne, the famous Carmel psychiatrist, assumed it was all right to bring a group of half a dozen or more of his patients in to show them how the other half enjoyed life.

For research on an article I wrote for the *Carmel Spectator*, I traveled up to San Francisco to check out the Beat Generation movement, and Pierre de Lattre's Bread and Wine Mission in the North Beach district. Most of this young bearded bunch, and their girl friends I interviewed, descended on us at the next Monterey Jazz Festival. Our lawn was covered with Fiats, Lambrettas, tents, and sleeping bags. They all returned, with more of their friends, the following Jazz Festival, and then the next. Out of desperation, I put up a high fence all around our property. On our locked gate, in Jazz Festival season, I tacked a sign:

BRUCE AND JEAN ARE OUT OF THE COUNTRY.
PLEASE DO NOT DISTURB THE TENANTS!!

Unlike Steinbeck's do-not-disturb sign on his Eleventh Street gate, ours seemed to work.

Just before the War, and about the time that John was posing for the oil paintings next door and Gwyn was complaining that Monterey was drab and provincial, I found myself broke and out of a job again. The big mural decorating jobs I'd been doing for Hotel Del Monte had suddenly ceased. I was sorry about that. They'd been fun and a challenge to do, and they paid very well. Mostly I'd constructed fantastic decorations for the big tourist convention parties. For example, one of the affairs was "Tortilla Flat Night," for which I'd built rows of shacks amongst a transplanted forest of pine trees, all around the perimeter of the dance floor of the huge Bali ballroom. Soon after this, due to the country's preoccupation with war work and the growing shortage of gasoline, Sam Morse, the head of Del Monte Properties, decided to discontinue the parties.

I took a job as a catskinner (a bulldozer operator) at the army construction project going on at nearby Fort Ord. It was miserable, hot, and grimy work. I would have felt sorry for myself, if I hadn't seen all the young draftees double-timing through the blinding dust around me.

Sam Morse decided to give one last party before the old luxury hotel was to be sold to the Navy for a "West Coast Annapolis." I heard he'd engaged Salvatore Dali, the famous Spanish surrealist, to design the final party, as a benefit for Hitler and Mussolini's bomb victims in Barcelona. The party was to be held over the Labor Day weekend. As I was off at Fort Ord, I asked Sam if I could work with Dali on the festivity. Since I'd done all the previous parties and knew the crew and where all the props were, he was happy to have me. I'd offered my services without pay, just for the experience of working with Dali, but Sam wouldn't hear of it. Nonsense! He'd pay me the same hourly wages as the rest of his crew!

It was a fabulous party. An unusual experience. Under Dali's direction we converted the Bali Room Ballroom into the Dali Room Grotto. From the ceiling we suspended thousands of gunny sacks filled with newspapers. Under the blue lights it looked like an enormous rockbound cavern lit by oblique rays of moonlight. The celebration was called "A Night in an Enchanted Forest." We brought in the transplanted pine trees from the Tortilla Flat Night party and built an extravagantly large bed for a dining table down the center of the grotto. Dali and his wife, Gala, in their night attire, hosted the banquet, their feet and legs under the tablecloth at the head of the bed. I'd made the head board from the two goal posts I borrowed from the Polo Field.

Dali spoke English only when he wanted to. I could speak a little Spanish. Bob Stanton, the architect, who'd been a classmate of mine at Berkeley, spoke a little French, and Herb Cerwin, the hotel's publicity director, spoke fluent Spanish, since he'd been raised in Cuba. Between the three of us, and with Dali's quick sketches, we figured out what he wanted. Down the center of the bed-table we placed autumn fruits, gourds, pumpkins, and cages of small wild animals. These consisted of live raccoons, opossums, porcupines, bobcats, and so on. Between each of the several hundred diners' chairs we placed a naked female clothing store mannequin. We removed the dummy heads and substituted fanciful papier maché heads sent up from Hollywood.

Dali came in about two o'clock each afternoon to see how we were doing. Most of the heads were of unicorns, leprechauns, and such fanciful creatures, but I'd just put on a rather caricature-like duck's head on one of the dummies when Dali arrived.

"No! No! Barooze! he exclaimed and snatched off the duck's head. "Eet's *demasiado* Valt Deez-knee!" (too much like Donald Duck?")

We placed a wrecked Model A sedan in the greenery with a nude girl asleep beneath it. She was an attractive artists' model, a neighbor of mine from Huckleberry Hill. We gave her so many sleeping pills that she slept through the entire party without moving an eyelash. I was a little leery about all the combustible material in the set. Revelers were never very careful with cigarettes. In case of a fire, I planned to dash out with my unconscious and rubbery nude neighbor draped over my shoulder.

The party went off well. Everyone seemed delighted

"Dali, ants & wilting watches"

In the 60s and 70s... Long after the canneries had closed down...

with Dali's strange surrealistic concoction. There were a good many famous names in attendance. Gloria Vanderbilt led the society group, while Bob Hope was the best known of the show business guests.

In the next few years, I saw Steinbeck only occasionally in Monterey, on some of his quick trips from New York. It was always in passing and never long enough for us to reestablish our old sense of camaraderie. At one time—in the very early sixties I believe—John had moved back to Pacific Grove for several months, but our paths didn't cross. The members of the Lab Club asked me if I'd invite John to one of our Wednesday night suppers. I refused.

"He might come and he might be charming," I told them. "On the other hand, he might be pretty nasty about it. Did you read that newspaper interview he gave last month to the effect that Ed's old Lab had been turned into a key club for a bunch of real estate Babbitts? He should know that's not true! You never know what to expect from him. Anyway, I'm not going to stick my neck out just so he can chop it off. Let somebody else bell the cat."

We dropped the whole idea. Not long after, one of our Lab members, Will Shaw, returned from a trip to Italy. He and his wife had been traveling on some sort of architectural fellowship grant. They'd met John and Elaine Steinbeck, his third wife, in a delightful little inn at Positano, south of Naples. The Shaws had introduced themselves and they'd dined with the Steinbecks that evening. Will said Steinbeck and his wife couldn't have been more genial. John was full of good humor and good stories, and Elaine was just as delightful. When they said farewell, John had told Shaw to be sure to give Jean and me his very best regards.

I felt rather chagrined when I heard that. I wondered if I'd been too stuffy in my judgment of John. Had he really mellowed that much? Perhaps because of his comfortable circumstances, his more than a decade of successful marriage, plus his now accepted position in the world of letters, he didn't feel the need to do battle with himself, and everyone else, the way he once had. I also wondered if I'd deprived that gang at the club of a once-in-a-lifetime chance to meet the illustrious John Steinbeck. John could be very impressive, when he was holding forth to a group, and great fun when he was in a pleasant mood, as he'd been on that trip to Baja, years ago. I decided that, if I had another chance to ask him to the club, I'd do it.

John was successful in his third and final marriage. John and his new love, Elaine (whom Jean and I have never met) were married in 1950—after John's second divorce, which, if possible, was messier and more traumatic than his first one. John later told Jean angrily that Gwyn had really set him up—taken him to the royal cleaners ("She charged two of everything at Tiffany's!"), before dropping the bomb that she was taking the kids and leaving him. She added insult to injury by implying it was for another man.

Toby and Marian Street, and others who met Elaine, told us John had finally "lucked out." John had always dreamed of a woman who combined intellect, culture, and good family, and our informants said she was all of these, and more. They said she'd been the former wife of Zachary Scott, the well-known actor, that she'd been in the theater herself, that John had met her while working on his screenplay, *Viva Zapata!*, and they both enjoyed the same things, particularly traveling. They also said she was an excellent step-mother to his two young sons from his previous marriage. In addition, she was remarkably protective of John in his continuing battle for privacy. What more could he ask for?

In 1962 Steinbeck received the Nobel Prize for Literature, winning out over sixty candidates from around the world. He Elaine, traveled to Oslo for the ceremony. The award was given for the sum of the author's life work, and Steinbeck certainly deserved the Nobel for that. It was also stated that his current novel, *The Winter of Our Discontent*, had been a contributing factor in his winning, because of its deep insight and fine writing. I couldn't agree with the committee's opinion on that one. With the possible exception of his previous novel, *The Short Reign of Pippin IV*, I thought *Winter* had been his most feeble effort.

During the 60s, John and Elaine were spending much of their time traveling in Europe, when they were not either in their New York apartment or at their seashore place in Sag Harbor, off Long Island Sound. John made one more extensive trip around America by himself, as research for his final book, *Travels With Charley*. He was quickly in and out of Monterey, and saw very few of his old friends.

His obituary said he died peacefully at his New York apartment, after a period of illness, on December 20, 1968. The death of the Nobel laureate made world-wide headlines and he was hailed as one of the century's most important novelists.

EPILOGUE

As a person John was often a conflicting puzzle. He could exhibit a number of opposing characteristics, either in rapid succession or at the same time. He could be irritable and cantankerous, or genial and long-suffering. Humble or overbearing. A man of calm vision, or one who was almost childishly fearful and superstitious.

For example, he gave all his Pulitzer Prize money from *The Grapes of Wrath* to Ritchie Lovejoy, fifteen hundred bucks, a lot of money in 1940. Ritch was an intelligent and gentle ectomorph, a disconsolate introvert. He always felt he was down on his luck. John thought the prize money would buck him up and encourage Ritch to finish a novel and long narrative poem he'd been working on, but I don't recall either being completed and published.

John never mentioned his gift—we only heard about it indirectly from Ed. It was generous and quite admirable. But then again, John could lecture members of the Lab Group peevishly, just for wasting their own money on two-bit lunches at the King Cafe.

I guess I'd always felt cheated somehow that Steinbeck had peaked so early in his literary career. When I knew him best, at the beginning, every book he wrote surpassed the previous one. I expected this to go on indefinitely. It didn't. After *The Grapes of Wrath*, I thought every book he wrote was less significant than the previous one, with minor exceptions. I figured John had slid off onto the wrong track and couldn't find his way back.

Of course, there are still a number of old-timers in town who profess to hate Steinbeck's entrails. One of these is Harry Noland, an eighty-three-year-old lawyer who represented the local Growers' Association back in the Depression days when Steinbeck's two controversial novels, *In Dubious Battle* and *The Grapes of Wrath*, infuriated the local establishment. Noland claims, in a recent quote from the *Los Angeles Times*, that he "won't give a penny" to the fund raising drive now underway for the new Steinbeck Center, which was originally proposed as a shrine-like adjunct to the John Steinbeck Memorial Library out on West San Luis Street. Now planners are saying the Center will be part of the refurbished Hotel Camino in the new downtown Steinbeck Plaza itself. Plans are going ahead, in spite of the opposition, as, apparently, there are fewer and fewer anti-Steinbeckers left alive each year.

It occurred to me recently that there is an interesting parallel to the life of John Steinbeck in the life of the Russian author Maxim Gorki (1868-1936). Gorki became famous as an anti-Czarist writer, living and working abroad at the turn of the century. Outside Russia, probably his best known work was his 1902 play, *The Lower Depths* which, like Steinbeck's *The Grapes of Wrath*, dealt with the poor and downtrodden social outcasts of his own native country. Unlike Steinbeck, however, Gorki was considered a popular hero in his own lifetime. He returned home after the Russian Revolution to the huge industrial city of Nizhni Novgorod, where he was born. This city had a population of about a million souls—some ten times the size of Salinas. In his honor, in 1932, the almost unpronounceable name of his home town (Knee-yezh-nyee, Gnaw-off-gur-rut) was changed to Gorki. Overnight he became the city's best known citizen. His name was on everyone's lips.

It is my personal opinion that John Steinbeck, our Nobel prize-winning author, being the only famous person ever to come out of Salinas (with the possible exception of the Smothers Brothers) will someday, like Gorki, give his name to his home town. There are many establishments in this area already named after him. (Finger your Yellow Pages!) There's the Steinbeck Library and the Steinbeck Festival. The Steinbeck Credit Union, the Steinbeck Mortgage Company, and, possibly to commemorate Steinbeck's somewhat exaggerated reputation as a two-fisted drinker, the Steinbeck Alcoholic Treatment Center.

As John Steinbeck's community standing becomes increasingly enhanced with the passing of time, it is my contention that the city of Salinas, California, at sometime in the near future will become Steinbeck, California.

For the last eight seasons, the Steinbeck Festival (held annually in the first week of August) has brought in from three to five thousand visiting tourists, as well as large numbers of fanatical literary devotees from all over the world. For their benefit, and since the city's name change seems inevitable in the long run, I believe we should do everything in our powers now to hasten the historical process.

Perhaps prematurely, therefore, I suggest that, instead of waiting around for gradualism and the inevitable, the change should be made now, today. A popular vote could do it, or perhaps a simple amendment to the city charter would suffice.

Let's change the town's plain old prosaic name of Salinas, California, to the glorious and significant new name of Steinbeck, California! And let's do it now, immediately, right away, *today*, if it's humanly possible.

And if Russo-American relations under Gorbachev's *Glasnost* continue to improve, what could be more appropriate then for Gorki-on-the-Volga to choose Steinbeck-on-the-Salinas as its Little Sister City in America.

INDEX

20th Century Fox 100
A Night in an Enchanted Forest, party 111
A Snake of One's Own, short story 5, 24
A Study of Genius, essay 93
A Thing That Happened 36, 62
A Week on the Concord and Merrimack Rivers 69
"About Ed Ricketts," essay 16
Academy Award 102
Albee, Dick 11
Alee, teacher 47
Alice in Wonderland 67
All Saints Beach 45
Amazing Stories, magazine 74
Anea, Sparkey 98
Ariss, Bruce, son 88
Ariss, Bryant, brother of Jean 89
Arnez, Desi 103
Asilomar 38
Austin, Mary 9
Bach 72
Baja 10, 14, 45, 49, 60, 76, 98, 99, 100
Bali Room Ballroom 111
Barcelona, Spain 110
Bear Flag Sporting House, Dora Flood 70
Beat Generation 110
Beau Geste, movie 51
Bechdolt, Fred 7, 9
Believe it or Not!, Ripley's 34
Belloc, Hillary 93
Benson, Jack, biographer 76
Berkeley 27, 34, 35, 40,
Berne, Dr. Eric, psychiatrist 110
Between Pacific Tides, book 19
Bierce, Ambrose, writer 74
Big Sur 34, 108
Boatworks, the 23, 72
Boodin, John 47
Bowen, Elizabeth, literary critic 104
Bread and Wine Mission, San Francisco 110
Broadway, New York 100
Bureau of Alcohol, Tobacco, and Firearms 26
Cal Tech 89
Cal, Berkeley 47
Call-Bulletin, newspaper 39
Cannery Row, 2, 3, 4, 13, 15, 19, 24, 26-27, 32, 81, 91, 93, 102, 103, 105
Cannery Row, book 3, 70, 76, 88, 92
Cannery Row, film 99
Carmel Hill 83
Carmel River 87

Carmel Spectator 110
Carmel Women's Club 86
Cerwin, Herb 111
Chaney, Lon, Jr. 95
China Point 23, 63, 72
Chong, Wing, grocer 70, 82, 107
CIA 108
Colletto, Tony 98
Columbia Pictures, Stanley Kramer Unit 102
Conger, Gwendolyn 95, 96, 98
Conrad, Joseph, writer 8
Conspicuous Waste, theory of 87
Corona Del Mar 41
Corral de Tierra 72
Covici, Pat, publisher 62, 97, 98
Covici-Friede 8
Crash, '29 .... 2, 40, 83
Crosby Gold Tournament 103
Crosby, Bing 103, 104
Crosby, Dixie 104
Cummings, Russ, photographer 19, 61, 104
Cup of Gold 4
Cymbal, newspaper, Carmel 79
Dali Room Grotto 111
Dali, Salvatore 110, 111, 112
Davies, Marion 37, 39
Dekker, Bill 92
Del Monte Bath House 13
Del Monte Express 105
Del Monte Park 88
Dennis the Menace 104
Depression 2, 29, 34, 43, 49, 67
Divertissement 72
Doaks, Mrs. Joe 108, 109
Dustbowl Okies 94
East of Eden 98
Edminster, Howie 35, 36, 56
Einstein, Albert 27, 53
Einstein, Fitch 89
El Camino Real 34
El Jusgado 51
Ensenada 53
Ernst, Old Pop, restaurateur 63
Esquire, magazine 5, 74
Father Serra 39, 80
FBI 108
Federal Writers Project (FWP) 7
Fisherman's Wharf 89, 98, 99
Fitch, Will 80

Fitzgerald, F. Scott	95
Flood, Dora, Bear Flag Sporting House	70
Fort Ord	110
Fort Ticonderoga	83
Frederick, Emperor, II, of Bavaria	78
Gabe, local character	76
Gabriel's horn	41
Gallatin's Restaurant	76
Garden of Allah	95
Gay, August Pierre François (Gus)	27, 28, 76, 78, 79
Gay, Marcelle	76, 79
Gilbert, Liza	79
Grable, Betty	96
Gragg, Mrs. Hattie	76, 77, 78
Graham, Barbara	98
Graham, Ellwood	99
Graham, Ellwood, artist	23, 98
Graham, Spike	104
Grapes of Wrath, The, book	2, 87, 93, 95, 99
Grapes of Wrath, The, movie	102
Greene, Sumner, architect	21
Greenfield	36
Gregorian Chants	72
Gregory, Sue, teacher	8-9
Grosssteinbeck	37
Hairy Ape, The	36
Hamilton	37
Harper's, magazine	5
Harris, Frank	95
Hearst, William Randolph	38, 39, 43
Hearst, William Randolph, holdings	37
Hedgepeth, Joel, writer	62
Heifitz, Betsy	105
Heifitz, Milt	92, 105
Herman, Hank	89
Herman, Suzy	80, 89
Hill 770	10
Hitchcock, Alfred	100
Hitler	37, 79, 110
Hokinson, Helen	108
Hollywood	100, 102
Hoover, President	49
Hopper, Jimmy	9
Hotel Cominos Coffee Shop	34
Hotel Del Monte	74, 110
Hovden Cannery	6
Huckleberry Hill	9, 11-12, 82, 84, 88, 103, 104, 105, 108, 111
I Love Lucy, TV Show	103
Ibert, Jacques, composer	72
In Dubious Battle, novel	2, 21, 28, 31
Italian Toscani, cigars	59
Jacks, Romey	83
Jackson, Helen Hunt, writer	44
Jackson, Toni Siexas	16, 92, 99
James, Henry, novelist	54
James, William, psychologist	54
Jeffers, Robinson, poet	39
Jeffers, Una	21
Jehovah	48
Johnny Bear	34
Johnson Ranch	67
Journal American, newspaper	37
Joyce, James	95
Jung, Dr. Carl	54, 55
Jung, theory	56
Kaufman, George	62, 83
Kennedy, John F., President	108
Ketcham, Hank	104
Killers, The, short story	35
King Cafe	80, 91
King City	36, 37, 39
Knotty Pine Inn	91
Kramer, Stanley	103
Krishnamurti, Hindu mystic	54
La Grange	84
La Ida	82
La Jolla beach	43
La Paz	99
Lab Group	11, 32, 54, 75, 72, 80, 88, 89, 91, 92, 97, 98, 107
Lab, Pacific Biological Lab	vi
Lannestock, Gustaf	90, 92
Larson, Evelyn Londahl	9
Late George Apley, The, book	93
Lattre, Pierre de	110
Lawrence, D.H.	104
Leidig's, store	8
Lenny, Steinbeck character	62, 100
Lewis, Sinclair	9
Lifeboat, movie	100
Lloyd, Marge	24, 32
Lockhart, Bruce, Lord Hamilton	92
Lockheed, Bruce	90, 91, 92
Lockheed, Jean	90
London, Jack	9, 104
Long Valley, The, collection	6
Los Angeles	40
Los Gatos	21, 61, 80, 83, 79, 93, 95
Lovejoy, Tal	24

Lytton, Lloyd ... 10
Marquand, author ... 93
Matthews, Al, attorney ... 93
McCullogh, Jock ... 83
Meredith, Burgess ... 95, 99
MGM ... 100
Miller, Henry ... 95, 100
Modern Man in Search of a Soul, book ... 54
Montague, Nellie ... 21
Monterey Bay ... 7
Monterey Beacon, magazine ... 4, 5
Monterey Jazz Festival ... 110
Monterey Peninsula ... 35
Monterey Piaisano ... 7, 9
Monterey *Trader* ... 75
Montez, Lola ... 78, 79
Moon Is Blue, The, movie ... 100
Moray eel ... 41
Morgan, Julia, architect ... 38
Moriarty ... 37
Morse, Sam ... 110
Moussorgsky ... 72
Mozart ... 72
Murphy, Dennis ... 104, 105
Mussolini ... 37, 69, 79, 110
New England Grand Banks ... 65
New Yorker, magazine ... 37, 103
Nickele, Nick ... 103
Night on Bald Mountain ... 72
Nobel Prize for Literature ... 113
North Beach, San Francisco ... 110
O'Neill, Eugene ... 36
Occident, magazine ... 81
Ocean View Avenue ... 4
Of Mice and Men ... 2, 62, 83, 95, 99, 100
Of Mice and Men, play ... 62
Okies ... 11
Oklahoma ... 76
Oklahoma, recording ... 109
Old Blue Diner ... 70
Old Man Bishop ... 11
Old Pacific Building ... 81
Olvera Street ... 41
Ott, Dr. Evelyn ... 54, 56, 84, 85, 86, 87
Ott, Peter ... 56, 84, 85, 87
Pacific Coast ... 21
Pacific Grove ... 3, 23, 80, 95, 102, 106, 112
Pacific Grove High School ... 3
Palace Flop House ... 70, 76

Parker, Dorothy ... 37
Pastures of Heaven ... 4
Pearl, The ... 99, 100
People's World, newspaper ... 79
Perelman, S.J. ... 103
Pie Wagon ... 75
Pilon ... 11
Pipe City, Berkeley ... 40, 41
Portrait of Jenny, movie ... 102
Preble and Nickele Realty (Monterey) ... 103
Presidio ... 10
Queen Charlotte Islands ... 107
Quick Years, The, novel ... 104
Ramona ... 44
Raspberry Flat ... 88
Ricketts, Alice ... 16, 105
Ricketts, "Doc" ... 15
Ricketts, Ed, Junior, ... 18
Ricketts, Nan ... 16, 56
Ripley ... 34
Rivera, Diego, art school ... 81
RKO ... 102
Rockcfeller-Terman, Stanford University study ... 92
Roosevelt, President ... 49
Salinas ... 3, 27, 34, 79, 84, 99
Salinas Valley ... 98
San Antonio ... 62
San Antonio del Mar beach ... 61, 62
San Diego ... 57, 65, 67, 68, 99
San Francisco Examiner, newspaper ... 100
San Jose Mercury ... 61
San Quentin ... 66
Santa Barbara ... 39, 40
Santo Tomas ... 51, 56, 58, 60
Santo Tomas range ... 53
Scott, Zachary ... 113
Scripps Institute Oceanography ... 41
Scripps warehouse ... 43
Sea of Cortez ... 98
Sea of Cortez ... 99
Seaside ... 11, 33
Second Coming ... 41
Selznick studio ... 102
September Morn, painting ... 65
Sergeant, The, novel ... 104
sex cult ... 100
Shakespeare ... 76
Shaky Tom (Old Shaky, The Pirate) ... 9, 10, 11, 12
Shane, Charley ... 11

Shanghai Low restaurant	91
Shaw, Will	112
Short Reign of Pippin IV, The, novel	113
Skahen, Rick, doctor	92
Snelling	84
Socrates	48
Something That Happened	36, 62
Spanish King's Highway	34
Spreckels Sugar Beet Factory	34
Standard Oil Company	39
Stanford Lit	35
Stanford,	15, 25, 27, 34
Stanton, Bob, architect	111
Steinbeck *Cannery Row*, book	3, 70, 76, 88, 92
Steinbeck *Cannery Row*, film	99
Steinbeck cottage	82
Steinbeck, Elaine	112, 113
Steinbeck, Gwyn	107
Steinbeck, John, photo	30
Steinbeck, John, son	88
Steinbeck, Thom, son	88
Stellar's sea cow	65
Sterling, George	9
Sternad, Rudy	102, 103
Sterne, G.B.	104
Stevenson House	27
Stevenson, Robert Louis	24
Stokes-Gragg Adobe	76
Strawberry Hill, (The Hill)	98
Street, Marian	113
Street, Peggy	89, 99
Street, Toby	25, 31, 89, 99, 105, 107, 113
Sweet Thursday	24
Tarbell, Ida M.	9
Teggart, Frederick, teacher	47, 48, 49
Terman Test Group	93
Termite	92, 93
Thatcher, Billy	73, 74
The Beacon	36
The Fairmont, San Francisco Hotel	96
Theory of the Leisure Class	87
Thoreau, Henry	6, 47, 69
Tiajuana	44
Tice, Rube, inventor	75
Time magazine	104
To a God Unknown	4
Todos Santos	45
Tortilla Flat Night, party	110, 111
Tortilla Flat, novel	7, 8, 11, 21, 23-24
Tortilla Flats, camp	9, 11, 38
Toscani cigars	60
Travels With Charley, book	76, 113
Travis, Tex	98
Treasure Island	24
Triumph Over Architecture, house name	13
Ulysses	95
University of Chicago	15, 47
Veblen, Thorstein	85
Verbeck, Pol	20, 26, 72
Viva Zapata!, screenplay	102, 113
Vuletich, Damo, artist	77
Walden Pond	69
Wall, Pat	89
Warren, artist	69
Watkins, Harlan, teacher	107
Wayward Bus, The, novel	99
Weird Tales, magazine	74
West Coast Annapolis	110
Western Flyer, ship	98, 99
Wharf Theater, Monterey	62
Wharf Theaters	100
What's Doing on The Monterey Peninsula	99
Whitaker, Francis, blacksmith	80
Winter of Our Discontent, The, novel	113
Withers, land owner	12
Woods, Flora, brothel (Flora's Place)	15, 19, 20, 70, 72, 73, 76, 82
Woods, Flora, Lone Star Restaurant	15, 70, 74, 76
Woolsey, Judge	95
WPA	3, 5, 7, 12, 49, 79, 82, 83
WPA mural	21, 75, 80, 82
Wyntoon Ranch	38
Yee, Jack, landlord	107
You Can't Take It With You, comedy	109
Zanuck, Daryl	102

For the sake of clarity we have left the following people out of this index: John Steinbeck and his first wife Carol, Bruce and Jean Ariss, Ed (Doc) Ricketts, and John Steinbeck's dog, Toby. Their relationship to the book is so intertwined that we felt their listing to be unnecessary.